UNIVERSAL IDEOLOGY EXPOSED

By John Grayne

Published by New Generation Publishing in 2022

First Edition

ISBN   978-1-80369-224-1

www.newgeneration-publishing.com

 New Generation Publishing

CONTENTS

CHAPTER 1 INTRODUCTION

IDEOLOGICAL THINKING IS UNIVERSAL

The new science of Linguistics has only been recognised for a few years. It shows humankind's universal ideological thinking has been the elephant in the room ever since we first spoke, which is now generally recognised, anyway in the west, as at least four hundred thousand years ago. Before, Scientific Linguistics was a Liberal Art. Now the elephant can and must be confronted and expelled. It may be that Professor Chomsky promoted his own work on Transformational Grammar to a science. Unfortunately there are other interpretations of what Linguistic Science involves. In October 2021 Professor Michael Hoey died, after a lifetime teaching modern English language sciences and how languages are learned. Once he had got his "lexical priming" worked out he taught it relentlessly; his obituary lists in forty countries, based at the universities of Birmingham and Liverpool in the UK. He was born in 1948.

In "Lexical Priming, a New Theory of Words and Language", published in 2005, he claimed to have transformed the understanding of how using words develops grammar. He was unmoved by Professor Chomsky's philosophical professionalism, at that time with an almost world-wide reputation at the Massachusetts Institute of Technology, MIT, who fancied our grammar came from our inborn instinctive thinking, at first even with a genetic element, although now it is generally accepted (as I also put it) speaking is not a process of any sort, like Darwinism for instance, a physical process, but merely an abstract whimsey, a human activity, our minds immaterial, an abstract term for our thinking, and before speech there wasn't much, it was like trying to do algebra without any symbols: you lost yourself. Our grammar needed priming, and this was from our lexical experience. Learning words and sentences as children (and originally humanity learning sentences in the first place) led to copying the grammatical patterns of words in sentences from one sentence to the next. A grammar is a network of sentences of words which primes our minds to the logical patterns common to them all. You could say we first made our words and then built a scheme of usage based on the commonality of the patterns of the sentences. We made the grammar up based on the sentences we were using. That was Hoey's message, his discovery or realisation, and now he is gone.

It could, I suppose, still be questioned how we knew how to order the words in the first place. But I think we will have just tried making sentences a randon (at random) at first to convey what we were thinking. Did we need to experiment how to think to prime our minds with the grammar of thinking then? Well if we did, we did; but if we did we had it done before we spoke.

By far the most interesting point so far as I am concerned is that the sentences came first, and the grammar was a subsequent construct, and indeed grammars of the complexity Chomsky enjoys formatting as his transformational grammar are a relatively recent construct.

When he composed his transformational grammar he was still a student at MIT. He had already embraced the Marxist dialectic; and quite apart from the determination with which he has maintained his linguistic dogmas into his old age, he has also maintained his political extremism, publishing political papers excoriating United States politics at every turn; and I have demonstrated the Marxist Dialectic is nonsense, a confusion of the boundary line and the continuum. Wokery has got to wake up and acknowledge this, and stop relying on it.

I feel I have gone behind the both of them, Chomsky and Hoey, when it comes to analysing the etymology and development of language. If grammar came from sentences putting together words where did the words come from so the sentences comprising them could be comprised? This is where I precede them both. The Origins of Speaking didn't have words. we learned how to utter merely single phonemes first, and the problem was how we were going to all discover the same single meaning for each different phoneme as it came burbling out of our mouths and we found we were all making the same sound. What was its meaning? We did not have any speech so we could not discuss the matter. We could only point and poke and keep using the same phoneme. What we needed was some directing principle to guide our thinking, so we would all be thinking along the same lines. What was it?

I fancy before ever we spoke we could make noises in our mouths and throats and we were poetic enough to copy the cuckoo with a "coocoo". The Ancient Egyptian owl said AaMahao (a lot better than Terwit terwoo). I can anger the barn owls flying round my house at dusk by whistling a very deep "a ma oo'oo", repeating every time they reply.

400,000 years ago, the sabre toothed tiger said GRRRR! I think Tarzan might have said Grrrr!, and I think it might have been taken to mean "I see, or hear, or smell a tiger, jump for the tall trees!". None of this speech was available, so you had to get the ideas just from Tarzan's copied growl. Those not quick enough in the uptake will have been eaten, so eventually all those left alive will have got the message, the survival of the fit enough and the deletion of the unfit enough in the prevailing environment; but not requiring any new species, just a quicker thinking attentive mind. There are those who will argue that these days with human speech our human evolution of species is superceded by our mental development, so we will develop mentally in place of evolving physically; but we are not concerned with any of that here, least of all as it could be used to nurture racism!

So far as I can see the only directing principle to get all our forebears' language committees thinking the same when they wanted the same meaning for all to adopt for each phoneme was the echoic principle: the noise we are making in our throats should mean whatever the same sound means in nature, the echoic principle. If anyone can think of any other principle available four hundred thousand years ago, they should please let me know it.

The only problem was, of course, even with echoism, the noises we were making in our throats didn't really sound all that much like the sounds we were accustomed to hear in nature. The symbolism required a bit of poetry. But that is not really the best way to put it. The natural sounds we picked were approximate. OK, there will have had to be a bit of pointing and repeating too; and of course it might have taken a thousand years or more! If it did, it did. We will never know. One way and another we got our echoic meanings together. What also came together was the realisation it was essential for all to stick to the same meanings, and not go wandering off, and if the correspondence with reality was not perfect that should be tolerated for the sake of maintaining the meanings. Once the idea was formed it could and should not be changed. Language was our first ideology, and we all adopted it at least four hundred thousand years ago, a time so long it is almost incomprehensible to the human intellect: for an Englishman it is 400 William the Conquerors or between 60,000 and 80,000 generations. For the United States of America some one thousand two hundred times as long as the United States. So ideology has got primed or printed in rather more than the child's grammar gets primed and printed in in only a few years. Well Hoey didn't say how long a single priming or imprinting took, and no doubt initially it wasn't as firmly primed as later his own grammar was. An ideology is more than a prime, many thousands of times more; and the ideological thinking imprimed by no means equates with reality. That is a sobering thought, and an important discovery.

When I wrote my first of three books on the discoveries of Scientific Linguistics, in 2006, I sent an article about it to Scientific American; but they rejected it because it was about language so they did not accept it was a science. Only a few years later they were publishing news of the new science of linguistics, although without much about its import. Well it was new. So of course they did not know much about it. I believe they still don't. Anyway, they are inclined to stick with the old sciences. There is much more of the old sciences, and there are many more of the old scientists to write about it, with things they are ready to write about. I have plenty to write about too, but I am writing another book about it, this one a political pamphlet for the specific purpose of dismissing all the Woke ideological fabrications now emanating from a leftist political Democratic (Socialist) Party in California under an elderly President Joe Biden, (whom I believe to have been a bit of an old woman even when he was young, as well as a Marxist) with Antifa, BLM, Cancel Culture, etcetera. now clinging to the Democratic Party fuselage there, with Wokery over all.

Linguistic Science has revealed that since we first spoke four hundred thousand years ago we have all of us been inclined to think in ideological terms, because language itself, and how we put it together, was itself an ideological exercise. Language was our first ideology and it still is.

In 2006, when I published my first book on linguistic science, academia all across the west, in Europe and America, was of the opinion we first spoke only forty thousand years ago, instead of the minimum of four hundred thousand years ago generally accepted in the west today. That is a big jump in fifteen years. A lot of time and effort had been spent on hunting for ash from camp fires in the stone age, because scientists believed it was after taming fire and establishing a warm environment outside the cave we had sat down and learned to speak. I believe that is likely correct, but ash eventually turns back into unburnt soil so they weren't finding it. The four hundred thousand years comes from ash found in 2017 six feet down under soil from tribal folk living at the back of a cave in South Africa. In my 2006 book, I had suggested it might well have been as long ago as six hundred thousand years, as a stimulus for rethinking the absurd forty thousand. But four hundred thousand years will do. It is so long a time it is hard for Sapiens Sapiens to get our minds around it. We had under-estimated the time it had taken us to develop language to where we are today by the thick end of four hundred thousand years; or look at it the other way about we had fancied we were ten times as smart and mentally nimble as we actually were and are; and we had picked up some very bad habits by the way, which I must now explain. In the rest of the world, apart from the west, as far as I know they have not gotten around to estimating when we first spoke at all; but if they had their guesses would no doubt have been just about as abysmal as ours.

The fact is the human mind's grasp of humanity's deep history is minimal. After all, we don't know much about it. But there are two deep truths to have come out of deep linguistic research, which were already in my first book in 2006; and they both concern the ideological thinking which has burgeoned in the last few hundred years, which appears to have come from Napoleon's ideology. He was a Corporal to start with, and enjoyed the absurd ideological conviction that France was the central power in Europe, and so it was therefore destined to dominate and rule Europe: it only needed first to exhibit the will to power and impose French dominance by force of arms. Accordingly, you could say he was the first Fascist, and all the other European Fascist states, Germany, Italy, Spain, France and Portugal all copied the ideology from him. Certainly Count Von Bismarck, who was the first copier, declared he had understood Emperor Napoleon's ideology, and so put the German statelets together with a zollverein or economic community, (like the EU), along with Prussian militarism; so in 1870 he was able to exert German will to power and attack and defeat France, marching his German troops down the Champs Elysée and under the Arc de Triomphe, to let the French nation know it was definitely the German state which was now "the central power" in Europe, not France at all; and it was therefore Germany which was destined to rule Europe. This ideology, in a German business-like manner was written up by the German military High Command, so all Generals would be fully cognisant of the strategic plan; and it is now known Kaiser Vilhelm had a copy of this paper too. Less well known is Hitler did as well. We do not know if the Franco-German Presidents who wrote the

European Coal and Steel Community Treaty in 1950, nominally to ensure France and Germany did not go to war again, but actually a Nazi plot now gradually transmogrified in seventy years into the European Union, still an unattractive national socialist conspiracy, knew of Bismarck's ideology too, but it seems likely they did; and what is certain is the EU constitution, with the Commission in Brussels has been word for word the same as the constitution written by Dr Goebbels in 1943 for Hitler's post-war "Thousand Year European Fourth Reich", ever since 1951, since it has been copied from the Nazi archive in Berlin again recently by Edward Spalton, Chair of the CIB, (Campaign for an Independent Britain), and when translated is word for word the same as the EU constitution. The democracy is only a pretence, the reality is the Commission governs Europe with the French and German Presidents the joint Dictators. This German ideology is thus the longest ideological (and Nazi) government to date. But many more ideologies now come raining down on us from all round the world and the one almost universally recognised is the Marxist one, which has played a prominent part in introducing all the others.

So now I want to go on to underline the two principal discoveries resulting from Linguistic scientific research, because they both concern the ideological thinking which underlies pretty well everything since Post Modernism in the west, (as well as everything before it, for hundreds of thousands of years, but we won't bother with all that now) so that virtually all politics nowadays is fraudulent and unthinking. Woke ideologies of one kind or another are leading to violence. The fact is all human thinking has been subject to ideology ever since we learned to speak, but humanity has nevertheless been unaware of the fact. If this ideological thinking is not shortly widely recognised and checked the various ideologies are likely to tear the world to pieces in due course. Deception and fraudulence are rendered universal because of the ideological thinking, and that makes all political movements turn to violence and indoctrination, just as Nazism did. The European Union is a classic Nazi ideology, deliberately introduced in 1950 by the French and German Presidents, both secretly still Nazi.

The first thing to come out of linguistic research is the truly astonishing fact that ideology is not just the evil philosophy of dictators like Adolf Hitler but the universal way all humans have thought ever since we first spoke. What is new is many more of us are taking to it - like ducks to water: I think because IT, the internet, gives us the knowledge base to put ideologies together and indeed the ability to promulgate them as well (think twitter, etc.).

The really astonishing discovery is our first ideology was language itself, and how we were able to get it started. We have been using it for four hundred thousand years, since we first spoke, and have been using ideology without knowing it, without knowing the nature of our own thinking. The fact is we still don't realise we are all ideological thinkers. It is part of human nature; and it is now urgent we should get wised up and understand the shortcomings of our own thinking because of our ideologies.

The second thing is we can begin to establish not merely the universal scope but the nature of ideological thinking. This is why I am writing this book now, and in a hurry. My linguistic research is my principal life work, but it is all done, and I am now old, and politics is not my principal interest any more. I have had a surfeit. But I suppose I have a duty to think of the interests of my grandchildren and subsequent descendants, along with all their contemporaries, and not leave them to sort out the ideological misunderstandings afresh after I am gone.

When you look at the wide spread of "Woke" ideologies today it is plain we are all addicted to ideological thinking, but all of us quite unaware of it; and this is because this is a discovery only of the latest science, Linguistics, and politicians are too busy, (and too vain), to spend time on what they will probably dismiss as mere philosophy, to avoid regarding it.

There have been three books called "The Age of Ideology" since the 1950s. I have read none of them, because they all presume ideology is an exceptional false way of thinking which does not concern ordinary people who are not victims of ideological indoctrination. In reality ever since we first learned to speak four hundred thousand years ago, we have all of us been inclined to get locked down in an ideological pattern of thinking while remaining completely unaware of it. It has not been just dictators. They have just had the nastiest ideologies. All the rest of us have been thinking in ideological terms. No indoctrination is required, so long as it is not patently outrageous and presented by a dictator in emotional terms. We all take to it like ducks to water. An ideology is just ideas presented in language with a belief attached, generally unwarranted, exaggerated and departing from common sense, but confirmed by the ideological thinking. This is the mischief. Ideological thinking can be novel, but it is always inward looking, and made up, and self-confirming.

The novelty can be compelling. It sent Archimedes out into the streets in his birthday suit, it was so compelling, to declare what he had discovered to everyone immediately. There was an element of impracticality there already. Who was going to pay attention to a scientific discovery confronted by a stark naked savant in the street obviously over excited. Carl Popper did it rather better. He edited his ideological thinking by thinking outside of it. It can be done, but it isn't, unless the ideology has been rumbled as false news. It has taken four hundred thousand years to get the understanding even started. Let us hope it will not take quite so long to get it generally understood.

It can be shown our first ideology was language itself and how we first set it up. We did it by adopting an ideology to get us all thinking the same. Come to think about it, without any language to debate the matter, how indeed were we going to get everyone to agree on the meanings of each one of the initial phonemes or individual syllables as we learned to utter them, without some form of indoctrination. These initial phonemes or single syllabic sounds are now our letters of the alphabet, now without any meanings, just the sounds so we can spell our words.

But there had to be some way we could get everyone to think in the same terms as we learned to utter each single syllable or phoneme. So far as I know there was only one way that it could be done. And even that was not easy. If anyone can think of another, do drop me a line. To get everyone thinking in the same terms there had to be some directing principle which would point everyone in the same direction, and this was tough because strictly there wasn't one. So we needed some ideological indoctrination to get us all thinking the same.

What is truly bizarre is nobody else on earth, so far as I know, has so far given this matter a moment's thought, ever since we had the same meanings for our first sounds as we learned to utter them. So how did we acquire language if there was no way we could all find the same meanings for the sounds? We needed a next best, and it came in the form of echoism, but it was a fanciful (ideological) echoism, which suggested each sound made with the human mouth had the meaning of the sound in nature it most closely resembled. So for example the sharpest phoneme Ka referred to the sharpest sound in nature which was considered to be the chink of chipping flints, which we had been hearing for a million years already. So Ka had the meaning of chipping flints. Of course we introduced meanings by gesturing, reiterating "ka" while pointing to the chipping; and then eventually in the same way for all the other phonemes in turn. Thus in due course "ka" came to mean too, depending on context, flint, strike, cut, hard and so on in a process of continual metaphorical enlargement of the coverage of the meanings.

The phonemes came to be pronounced in strings (words) to increase the differentiation of meanings, and give them more use. Then the words became nuggets with their own meanings, their derivations from their constituent elementary phonemes forgotten. A few years ago now the English dictionary acquired its millionth word, each with its own meaning or meanings. Every one had acquired the meanings by a continuous process of metaphor after metaphor from the original meaningful single phonemes, and this has been going on for four hundred thousand years. We don't have any direct recollection of it for more than the last ten thousand years or so at most, generally more like just five, but we have been able to establish how we have expanded our vocabulary during that time, by metaphor after metaphor.

My 2006 book had a chapter on each original phoneme and the original meanings that were ascribed to each of them, as well as how the meanings then enlarged. And so do the other two books I have written since on linguistics, but this one I am now writing is not on linguistics it is political, and we have done with the linguistics, merely using the research to explain the way we have all adopted ideological thinking. Now we must address the universal ideology resulting, which is making fools of us all; and you should get at least the gist of this confusion in pursuit of our universal ideological thinking which is here revealed.

Before moving on, the same arguments apply to the development of any language. These phonemes are not English phonemes, there weren't any languages when the meanings of the first phonemes were being established. It was four hundred thousand years ago.

In this chapter I intend quite unscrupulously to borrow some of my homework from my first linguistics book, so I can have my original analysis of Marx's dialectic and start by demolishing here again this leading ideology. I have demonstrated - nobody else has - that the Marxist dialectic is simply a mistake, confusing two different lines or distinctions as if they were the same. Once you have got this distinction clear the dialectic simply disappears, having fooled everyone for nearly three hundred years. I have myself been thinking about it on and off ever since 1940, when at school I was taught by my history teacher Robin Gordon-Walker, the younger brother of Lord Gordon-Walker, Clement Attlee's Foreign Secretary, whom he ennobled. Both brothers were Marxists, which the Prime Minister didn't mind. Lord Gordon-Walker was a rather ordinary European history teacher too until summoned to higher service. He wrote a short school book on modern European history which brother Robin saw we all had to buy and study from in prep at nights. At fifteen we were whizzers at recounting the dialectic. But teenagers don't stick with any ideas for long and while still sixteen we had moved to another teacher, Raymond Carr, later head of St Katherine's College at Oxford, a political think tank, for 20 years, and Sir Raymond. He reached 93. We remained friends. When he taught us he had Masters degrees from Queen's College in Oxford and Heidelberg University in Germany, which he was just able to complete before war broke out. (The universities mostly ignored Nazism).

We really need this demolition of the dialectic here because I want to include in this chapter too the explanation of all ideological thinking, which we all suffer from, and have done ever since we first spoke, and its shortcomings; which will perhaps stop Harry and Meghan in their ludicrous tracks and at the very same time very much improve international affairs with a similar type of correction of all the other ideological thinking coming out of the USA today. To appreciate the effect of universal human ideological thinking you need to have some understanding of how language began, which is how I discovered it myself in the first place. It took me the thick end of thirty years. It should hardly need thirty minutes to follow the business through here now.

The thirty years of debate with myself enabled me to establish the scope of ideology, because it is simply the way we all think and have thought ever since we learned to speak. Our first ideological thinking in fact was how we set up language itself – how we were able to put it together. When you come to think about it you realise that up until now nobody else has addressed these issues, because the intellectual establishment, a world bunch of professors all tidily wrapped in their ideologies, came to the common conclusion it was too difficult, impossible in fact. I ignored other thinkers, profs and all, as absurd; and it turns out I was right.

Before we spoke, our thinking was quite modest because all we had to give us terms to think in was what we saw. We must have thought solely in pictures, having no words. You can argue we must have thought in ideas, but our ideas can only have comprised the pictures of what we saw. What else? I am not wanting to deny we have abstract ideas today, but I question if we had them four hundred thousand years ago when we hadn't a word. I think the abstract ideas were, as it were, squeezed out of language in the course of time, which was in turn an enormous increase in mental activity, our thinking. You have to allow that the building of a vocabulary of words from the utterance of the first phonemes (single syllables) may have taken thousands of years. We certainly didn't just learn how to pronounce the first phonemes and everyone came walking out chatting. It was a lengthy development, but in no way an evolution. Evolution only refers to biological development, as Charles Darwin described it, although nowadays the word is debauched and may be referred to changes in the design of cars or even of philosophies. The development of ideas is a human whimsey, unguided by any process, and certainly not by our genes. The ideologies are part of the whimsey.

An ideology is a limitation of human thinking. Both sciences and religions are ideologies, just as Nazism and Communism and Chairman Mao's lucubrations are. The particular ideologies are not all evil in the same way as these social ideologies were, but they do suffer from some of the same mental characteristics, and that is the point of my book, to get these shortcomings understood by the users, particularly the not inconsiderable numbers in the USA now stuck with the Marxist dialectic, and worse all the other absurd ideologies society is stuck with all across America. It is hard to know which to pick on first. Antifa leading out of Marxism, along with wokery and BLM, and Cancel Culture, which I am told have even affected some professors in Californian universities, and the Democratic Party (Socialists) led by the new (but physically and mentally fading) president Jo Biden, with Cancel Culture growing out of the others like an intellectual cancer – because that is what an ideology is, an intellectual pattern which repeats itself and makes any other thinking wrong. You can see this even with a professor of science. The unscientific is wrong in his case. If it were only Professors of Science who allowed themselves an ideology our political world would be different. Unfortunately, it is the wholly unscientific who pick up ideologies to equip themselves with a substitute for understanding, in order to bolster their self-confidence. It gives them a bogus intellectual Satnav to go by. When almost everyone is at it, it results in more or less universal intellectual misunderstandings and fraudulence. Nothing is straightforward any longer. You find the Duchess of Sussex on TV claiming that to make up your own idea of what is true is actually correct, because there is no objective truth. That was the ideology of a not very bright German

Socialist Herbert Marcuse way back in the 1930s, which is nearly a hundred years ago, when Nazism too was widely believed in Germany too, and ideologies were not understood as they are now.

The Duchess is not a German historian and so can only have picked it up from Antifa in California, and thereupon copied on air without a qualm. Antifa picked it up, no doubt, as handy when setting out all the targets they wanted to choose for their violent ideology. Nobody with a fully sane and educated mind can believe the theory there is no objective reality so you can make up your own truth today. It was dismissed over fifty years ago by the Cambridge philosopher Wittgenstein, who originally came from Austria, and concluded "The world is what it is, and not another thing". He wasn't a Marxist with his mind messed up before he came to add his own ideological absurdities to the pile. What is the peculiarly unintelligent bit is to conclude there is no objective reality but nevertheless your private truth should be accorded the objectivity just the same as if there were. Wittgenstein could debate with Bertrand Russell whose mathematical book copying the title of Isaac Newton's is behind the development of linguistic science today.

Before we spoke, it is challenging to think in what terms we thought. It must surely have been in pictures, what we had seen or what we might see. The trouble must have been that we had no way of remembering what we had been thinking so we could rejoin our line of thought and add to what had occurred to us before, or amend it in any way. It strikes me the thinking will therefore have been quite difficult, with no verbal record in our heads to get back to, so I believe not all that much thinking got done until we spoke. I think before we spoke the fact is we were without much thought. Language speeded us up no end, so now we are effectively a different species, supposedly Sapiens Sapiens in place of dumb single Sapiens, both otherwise cases of the same Homo Erectus species.

The origins of thinking and language, and their pursuit has always been recognised as closely related. The development of one has obviously gone hand in hand with the development of the other. Indeed it has sometimes been argued the one has simply become the obverse of the other. Generally it is proposed (wrongly) advances in thinking mirror advances in linguistic achievement: when we find words for new ideas then we start to think in terms of them. Well we do, but somebody must have had the idea first. You don't have a word without an idea. In the same way, most people imagine they think in words - probably because when they come to express what they think it comes tumbling out in words. Of course Wayland Smith has always learned the words others have put in place. But thinking in words is only shallow thinking, the original thought is prior. Worse, all education is in words (even when accompanied by still pictures or movies - or mathematical symbols), so that education tends, willy nilly, to reinforce the illusion and keep students thinking at a shallow level, often doing no more than building their vocabulary, (more or less erudite depending on the quality of the education). My books have tried to get anyone reading them to think much more in terms not dictated by the language they happen to speak but in terms of the prior terms in which we first spoke, the semantics - not because the semantics were better, they weren't, but because they are explanatory of a good deal that is wrong in our current thinking, particularly our universal ideological bias, which comes from our primitive lingo, and has gravely damaged the last few hundred thousand years of dumbed down progress, and still damages our thinking today with absurd ideological beliefs.

Of course our ideological bias keeps folk politically correct (PC) as well. The lexicon can in fact function as a very efficient pair of political blinkers, to the conscious mind at least, leaving only the subconscious to its original native untrammelled perceptiveness and lack of inhibition or judicial stricture.

Moreover the recent explosion of information, crying out to be mastered, due to explosions in the media, principally the technological and scientific media, most importantly the internet, has only reinforced this shallowing of thinking. If you have to be well informed, or only apparently coping even, you had better not spend too much time on questioning methodology or exploring epistemological issues. You may not even learn these terms, so busily are you encouraged to attend to informing yourself and memorising names, data, formula, etc. adding them to your basket. Students, if their wits are about them, wish for time to digest and mull over all this intellectual pabulum, and if they are enthusiastic may conspire to give the syllabus another twirl after qualifying. The retake of course has to go by the board later. Some even drop out bemused by the absorption rat-race, judging themselves inadequate, or at least in some way not cut out for academic success. In some ways they are the saner ones. Academics, meanwhile take the dropouts as evidence of natural selection and see no need to question academic procedures.

Also there are very few poets left. They are increasingly seen as dropouts or comical rhymesters, and nowadays they probably are. In Victorian times they were still revered as the deepest thinkers, and they probably were. There are no Lord Tennysons today. With inspiration there is still a struggle as we grope for words to formulate and express the ideas we perceive, whether dimly for the most part, or just occasionally with a sudden "Eureka!" feeling as if a veil were lifted and we suddenly got a flash vision of the reality such as sent Archimedes out into the street in his birthday suit. But nowadays education is no longer treated as a personal struggle for understanding. It is presented as accumulating public knowledge towards certitude and certification, so the competent can feel competent and right, with charity towards the less well equipped for this if they hesitate. This is simply wrong and misleading in every particular. It is "Red Brick" learning in the most pejorative sense. We finish up with the reduction ad absurdum of a well stocked memory, the badge of a shallow thinker, treated as a master mind and given a glass trophy.

Surprisingly, feminism, which might have been expected to provide some check on the male tyranny of the word, has had the reverse effect. Feminists, thinking of themselves as counter attackers, have moved into male territory arguing they can think like males just as well as men. They can of course, (perhaps with some upset to their feminine hormone balance, who knows?), but it is not what is wanted from them. The female mind is the one free from male intellectual and linguistic hangups, although there is a view, indeed a probability, that women were originally the instigators of linguistic advance at the origins of speaking, using their articulation to massage the egos of their male partners − I guess in return for meat and sex. They remain natural talkers, still massaging, without falling themselves for lingualism, perhaps knowing perfectly well it has been a mild fraud from the beginning. For the males, meanwhile, speech is ego-massage. Their "objective" subject matters are easily appropriated as extensions of the self. So they get a double ration, their own and their partner's massaging and attention.

Still, it has to be said, men are natural go-getters, and as such they have powered progress ever since our hominid ancestors came down out of the trees, whether the girls care to admit it or not. There is nowadays, after hundreds of thousands of years, more in language than merely feminine charms. It is a whole new world of substantive conceptualisations. It is not that the female mind is less capable of contributing to human science; simply that they have not cared to pursue the matter until recently, and the male mind has thought to encourage them in this.

Feminists may wish to interject here that the males have unfairly cut them off from education and stunted their intellectual development over millennia, in extension of their first mischief of similar effect, impregnation. It would be idle to deny these charges; but most of the time the girls were happy to concede. They just wanted babies, like their mothers before them, before anything else. If they hadn't would the human race have survived? Now they are beginning to think they can find something better to add to motherhood, or indeed more tidily to precede it.

After these preliminaries, without wasting any more time it seems appropriate to address the kernel of human ideologies, the dialectic. It turns out the dialectic is in fact relict of some of our earliest ratiocination. One of the earliest symbols scratched on rocks is the Tau or letter T. It is found with circles and spirals. which appear to express nothing much, perhaps the mental confusion from the lack of any meaningful symbols to express thoughts churning about inside their heads in the absence of language. If that is the case it illustrates the intellectual nausea which obtained before we learned to speak. We were claustrophobic, sticking spears into animals and each other. I think it must have been something of a nightmare to be alive. The Tau comprises a vertical and a horizontal stroke and they have been as it were married together. You could surely argue the horizontal line represents spatial extension, the view, the world (which was supposedly flat). Then the vertical extension is change, or as we would say time, pushing the world into movement and change of scene. Admittedly, it isn't quite how things actually happen, but it does seem to be what our first thoughts might have amounted to, trying to find and record a pattern of events to grasp, and understand as reality. Nobody would have scratched the Tau repeatedly for no reason at all. It took a time, and used up a sharp flint. It clearly was regarded as a matter of some importance whatever it was. What I find another matter of equal importance is it also seems to correspond to the stage when we were inclined to count one, two, both of them, in short before we had added the idea of iteration: so that we could count one, two, three and so on; because it is this stage which first introduces the making of the dialectic as the pattern of our thinking when we began to speak. This is why I have named the Ancient Egyptian three vowel system the Tau Oon. The Oon is just the one or unity. Their vowels were aaa, iii, and ooo; with the e and o of our five vowel system coming later, e from ai and o from au. (I am of course well aware that in many different languages today there are innumerable sub-vowels which don't fit this pattern particularly well, I just don't think they disqualify my vowels. They merely add to them).

I have no need to repeat my chapters on the vowels here, where the particularisation of the meanings of the vowels follow a quite specific dialectical pattern. So the dialectic (thesis, antithesis, synthesis, or one, two, both of them) was a pattern of our original speech, and yet still guides our dialectical thinking today to a degree which is quite unconscious, and regularly disastrous.

The dialectic is a term based on the Greek for dialect or conversation, or perhaps better, as used for the dialectic, argument. First interlocutor A has a go declarative of his thinking; and then B states a different idea, with the (astonishing) result that (like the tau) the two ideas become combined as a third stage, in combination. So these stages are represented by the Greek terms "thesis, antithesis, synthesis", ("proposition, opposing proposition, combined proposition") making an automatic process, which can be applied to the real world and how it goes, and also to the machinations of the human brain, how human thinking goes too. There is a corollary here: if the dialectic is how the world proceeds, then those thinking dialectically will be thinking right and those not thinking dialectically will be thinking wrong! Stalin killed all he thought he could see were thinking differently to him because they must be traitors thinking non-dialectical thoughts, else they could not differ. As no two persons think identically, it did mean he killed really a lot of people, and quite rightly according to his dialectical thinking. His executioner, Comrade General Bobkin in the KGB, has recently died at 100. He said of the hundreds, no thousands he had had shot when Stalin told him to: "they weren't dangerous but they were enemies of the people". It was in his obituary in the UK. Well, after all, if you were thinking outside the dialectic you were a mischief at best. It was a commonplace of communism.

I should now make it clear I believe the whole scheme of Marx's and Hegel's dialectic is absolute rubbish, based on a complete misunderstanding of human thinking, and I now intend to demonstrate as much beyond a peradventure. This had never been done before I worked it out, which is why the dialectic has been able to survive and has acquired so many followers over so wide an area and for so long a time. Critics have disagreed with all the outcomes of this thinking, because they can be very extreme. But that has not put off those who have once got the pattern into their heads, who are basically simpletons who are quite unaware, for instance, a line is not a singleton but can mean different things; so the dialectic skips from one to the other kind of line to enable their non sequiturs to appear to be sequiturs. I don't mind admitting I am rather pleased with this intellectual analysis, which was lengthy and hard work, destroying much of the politics of the last three hundred years as balderdash. I can not say the next three hundred will be much better, in spite of my homework, since the aficionados of the dialectic will, first, refuse to read a heresy, second fail to understand it if they do, and thirdly decide to stick with the good old ideology anyway. I am afraid that is how ideologists react to all contradictory information. If it does not fit in with their ideology it can not be right, you see. This is why the progress of science (knowledge), over the last few hundred thousand years has been so abysmally slow: professors, the ideologists of the day, have stuck to their ideologies which have all been wrong (incomplete). Science has a long history of believers refusing alterations introduced by newer and better thinkers and sticking to the good old scientific ways because the new theories can not be accommodated in their existing ideology. I am not wanting to suggest current professors are all of this calibre; although apparently some appear to be, because some professors in universities in California are reported to follow the 1930s German

Socialist philosopher Herbert Marcuse who said "there is no objective truth, only your own individual truths, what you believe to be true". Although this kind of silly conceit, handy if you want to make stuff up, was dismissed fifty years ago by the rather difficult Austrian philosopher Wittgenstein, who said "The world is what it is, and not another thing", it has been resurrected by the extreme left Marxist ideology calling itself "Antifa" (Anti-Fascist) which has grown up in the USA in the last twenty years and is related to wokery, BLM and Cancel Culture. They all take advantage of their Marcusian ideology to follow their own truths, without needing any justification whatever. Anyone wanting to get any understanding of the implications of these ideological orientations should certainly read the recently published book "Unmasked" by the US journalist Dr. Andy Ngo, (originally by birth Vietnamese whose parents could take no more Vietnamese government Marxist totalitarian ideology and fled to the USA. When Antifa realised he was hostile their response was to kill him in a street protest, by hitting him on the head with a metal bar after knocking him to the ground and then kicking him unconscious. But he recovered against the odds, and eventually came out of hospital after six months and with astonishing bravery disguised himself in Antifa's Black uniform from head to foot, including with mask, joined their protests and has published all their street tutorial papers for killing policemen and establishing their Marxist/Anarchist ideology, exposing their mad thinking. Meanwhile they are repeatedly burning cities all across America as I write. Everyone involved in politics in the United States, and indeed elsewhere, should certainly read this book "Unmasked". The many Remainers in the UK who refuse to give up subservience to the Nazi ideology in the EU should read it too.

My book is meant to explain how ideology is the normal thinking pattern of humankind, and has been ever since we learned to speak some 400,000 years ago; so the Woke ideologies in the USA and UK are no more reliable than Hitler's Genocidal Nazi ideology. Ideological thinking inevitably leads to illusion at the same time as a vastly increased belief in it, because all ideological thinking is inward looking and thus self confirming. It includes both science and religion, which are classic ideologies, as well as the ideological political beliefs, Hitler's and Woke's.

Antifa, BLM, Cancel Culture and Wokery have been gifts from the USA to the UK with their racist issues, I understand 38% of the US population are not white, and the ones originally native in Africa (we can guess their skin colour but must not define them by it) have a lively recollection of the slavery which brought them there. Antifa came to the city of Bristol on 24 March 2021 when a small mob attacked a police station, burnt a police car (with 2 officers trapped inside); while BLM has toppled statues and even painted Winston Churchill because he respected the British empire, now the Commonwealth, which never had a slave, only the Caribbean and the American rebels did, which clearly makes for ideological confrontation; and everyone born alive over the last 400,000 years since we learned to speak has been and is an ideologist. Offer anyone an ideology and he will naturally respond, unless it has codicils he strongly opposes. It is not logical, it is ideological, just like Comrade General Bobkin's thinking, and it can therefore be just as mistaken.

Anyway the dialectic is our Lithic heritage, a nice example of our first linguistic thinking. It is an irony the Communist dialectic proves to be an atavism and not a novelty at all.

Jumping many millennia, Klaus Fuchs (the atomic spy) sold out the UK, his adoptive country, his family, and lastly even his tennis club cronies because of the dialectic which as a nuclear scientist he had to believe was prior even to science, which after all is a verbalised discipline, because the dialectic was pre-linguistic and so could claim to be based on pure unadulterated thinking – which actually, of course, is savage. So he followed Marx's dialectical thinking and gave the science of the west to the Russian ideologists, similarly wrapped in the Marxist dialectic and ideology. This is really quite surprising. Fuchs was clearly no fool in conventional terms. He had scientific Chutzpah. He was a practicing atomic physicist.

So why did he do it? No doubt his psyche wanted to posture against the everyday. That will have helped him study leading edge science too. But his mistake is a testimony to the power of the dialectic, which has always been perceived - ridiculously - as deep thinking, prior to all the methodologies which utilise speaking, and in particular prior to all scientific methodologies, something a priori and given, so you can't argue with it.

There is some merit here in being able to trace the dialectic far back into human history. It can be used as a credit, as nothing new. Ancient Egypt already reveals it as an ancient piece of established mystery. Across Europe the dialectical way of thinking is still believed today, at least in decadent academic circles, I believe particularly in France. Even in China the spell also persists, in spite of their otherwise very different language idiom. It is to do with moral justification. If benevolence and beneficence still appear to be tied up with dialectical thinking then that is the way academics are inclined to think; historical evidence or even reason notwithstanding. Plato (550 BC) used dialectical methodology to argue moral cases, basing his approach on Socrates who in turn proclaimed his debt to Egypt. But the alternate toing and froing of the dialectical process is thousands, even hundreds of thousands of years before both of them as well as the Egyptians. We might just mention here Ancient Egyptian thinking has had

to be entirely resurrected along with the
Egyptian language, because the Wahabi Moslem
Khaliphait's genocide resulted in the loss of
much of the Egyptian cultural heritage as well as
all their language. It is a permanent cultural
disgrace the Muslim community must bear, from
early days when the Khali-phai, or Caliphate, the
prehistoric Black Goddess Khali's followers,
only pretending to be followers of The Prophet,
killed all the Ancient Egyptians so the language
and much of its culture was destroyed and by
force of arms fought their way all along the north
African coast of the Mediterranean sea into
Spain, genociding the populations as they went,
so Spain was then forced to be Islamic for 300
years.

In early Aramaic, the sole language of both
the Prophet Jesus and the Prophet Mohammed,
Khaliphai means Khali-worshiping or Kali-
worshipers, and does not mean followers (of The
Prophet Mohammed) as the Kaliphate pretended
as they subverted Islam, the all merciful religion,
with a campaign of warfare and genocide all
across north Africa into Spain. The prehistoric
Black Goddess Khali, goddess of the night, of
Death, Destruction, Deception and all things of
the dark, worshipped by the Quereishi tribe of
Mecca, before The Prophet Mohammed rescued
them from their idolatry, had a renaissance after
the Prophet's death, still not recognised by
Islam. It was Khali who promised any of her
followers, who killed fifteen unbelievers in Her,

seven virgins in the hereafter. The virgins are fraudulent, but indicate Khali-worship to this day, so Osama bin Laden was a heretic and Khali worshipper, whether he knew it or not. Their tribal warfare was hardly ameliorated because the Khali-Phai kept some of the Ancient Egyptian mathematical achievements as theirs. It was far worse than the Akkadians' attack on the Sumerians a few thousand years previously. The Akkadians were primitive Semites, as indeed the Egyptians were too originally, as they were Akkadian adventurers farming the African tribes, initially in the Nile delta, after invading across Arabia and the Reed Sea, teaching the African tribes irrigation as they had learned it from the Sumerians who brought the skill from Eastern Malaya, (the Garden of Eden), when the Adamites were driven out when the world sea level rose 160 feet with the melting of the ice, piled a mile high over some of the earth, at the end of the last Ice Age (so far) - and we don't know why it ended or began. So it might be back any time.

Now we must get down to the analysis of human thinking and polish off the dialectic, and analyse all the other ideologies. So what are the original categories of human thinking? Indeed, prior to that, what is a category – of thinking or anything else? These questions need answering succinctly and with complete clarity if any progress is to be made in clearing up the misconceptions of the last four hundred millennia.

First of all mental perception is fundamentally dictated by our visual sense – it has been described as the tyranny of the eye, the only non-reflexive sense we possess; all the others (feeling, temperature, pain, taste, in practice hearing even) are personal experiences, reflexive, but vision is of the world around, and therefore purporting to be objective. The panorama, all that can be seen, the visible scene, is the local phenomenal world. The supposedly objective world of objects is given by the eye. Perhaps we trip over it sometimes too, but the pain of stubbing the toe is clearly subjective.

So now we must pause to see what is involved in seeing, and what ideational constructs it entails. Infants open their eyes and learn to focus them. What do they see? Focus brings to attention distincta. Perhaps the infant is seeing the wallpaper in the nursery. Let us suppose it has a floral pattern, with red flowers on a contrasting ground. With focus, the eye will pick out the contrast at the boundary between a flower and the ground. The mental event is best represented as "Distincta!" or rather let us say "d!", for "See!" in English, and also for "Distinction!" (d!). The eye will follow this distinction and will trace out a boundary and so eventually – in a day or two only – realise there is a bounded area (the flower). The bounded area so identified is indeed a category, d', (d dash) first the category, the "Red" area (though red may not discriminate colour as yet, just what happens to be there, inside the enclosure, which is red), later perhaps also or instead the category "flower", or finally "red flower" and "rose", but certainly not yet.

The pivotal point needs to be underlined that the category is derived indirectly from a prior and more elementary identification of a simple distinction or boundary, because from the very same distinction (d!) come the pregnant identifications of (d'), "Red" and "Not-Red" on either side of the category's boundary line, and this already has relevance to the Dialectic, as we shall see.

We might tease our understanding of the Dialectic at this stage, debating if this "Not-Red" is the opposite of "Red" or if the "Not-Red" is merely the absence of red. We are going to need to be able to recognise the difference between the absence of a property and its opposite if we are to see through dialectical thinking, which confuses them. It is already a challenge to the many potent grave and reverend intellectuals who have not thought in these terms and remain confused by the Dialectic to this day. But then they do not concern themselves with infants whom they probably think of as mewling and puking merely. But it was they who introduced our thinking. We did it, after we were born. Who else?

The original discrimination (d!) - exemplified by distinguishing a change of colour on the nursery wallpaper (but just as well the aureole of an erect nipple for those who fancy a psychologically marked target as trigger – can be represented conceptually as a simple line or boundary. Flower and nipple boundaries are in fact curvilinear of course but the simplest representation of a boundary is an unmarked one, which simply continues, and so is just a line, and so a straight line. This is the stage characterised above as d! As the distinction suggests a distinction-between, no doubt prompted by a flower or nipple pattern which goes on round to enclose reasonably neat targets, the single boundary line then bends round both ways in the mind to convert the boundary idea to a category, matching more or less the way the eye follows d! around the periphery, until it finds itself isolating not one but two categories, red and not red. This is probably the source of the butterfly patterns scratched on stone, the acme of Stone Age thinking vouchsafed in triumph to posterity.

Archaeologists have identified these scratches as a butterfly or even a double headed axe, giving a simplistic interpretation to a symbol invented by minds supposedly simplistic. The point is the two categories or butterflies' wings, d', red and not red, are mentally developed from a single discrimination (d!) and they all three appear in the glyph. Purists may wish to challenge the double whammy implicit in my figure-of-eight pattern developed from a single category, the butterfly design, showing this dual categorisation from a single boundary identification as sufficient to summon its negative to mind; but I am unmoved by them. We are not talking about a stage which can take in a substantive item on a ground, and the objection is therefore anachronistic. After all if a line merely curls round in the mind will it curl right or left? Obviously it can equally go either way and so it will go at one time one way and at another the other way, so it ends up going both ways; the symmetry of an unmarked mind indeed demands it as sweet reason. So along with our category we get a phantom doppelganger whether we aim for one or not. What are these two? In our example they are "red" (or for the nipple deep browny pink) and "not red" for the ground of the wallpaper (or not-so-browny pink, for the breast): which we can now write in generalised form as "x" and "not x", universals. If I am right this is an important stage in the development of human rationality. The ability to shuck off the evidence of our senses when false similarities, (such as the moon and cheese!), are presented, so that we are freed from the tyranny of the eye, comes only very many millennia later - if at all.

Meanwhile it has been our misfortune to have another line in our minds, which we have readily confused with the first one, the criterion, the awareness of a differential marker. It is known nowadays as a continuum. Let us call it c! There is no language which does not recognise the notion of more, though in earlier language it was sometimes clumsily expressed. Mathematicians, concerned with numbers, mix it up with next these days. It is in fact a difficult concept to get across, as primitive concepts go. Computer buffs as well as symbolic logicians and simple mathematicians too will recognise the greater than sign >. Because it is greater, from left to right (the direction of the script) the lines converge, reducing their spread, imaginatively to equal a following sign of ordinary size.

Contrariwise, the "lesser than" sign opens out from left to right so that the initial diminished spread leads to an expansion to catch up with a virtual term on the right of standard size.

These terms deserve serious mathematical consideration. The initial term on the left of an equation would have to contract or expand in those ways to equal the term on the right in other words. It is clear "greater than" and "less than" are relations developed (logically) from the middle case of equality or "same" although the original perception probably hardly encompassed this sophistication, coming from a perception somewhat more akin to "What a Brama! You don't see many wide mouthed frogs with mouths that wide these days!" Here we were simply grading things, (as to size or perhaps as to weight – we shall never know). It is hard to get behind these ideas. The relationship is mathematised as a gradient and formulated in mathematical symbols in various ways. But we can surely see today the conceptual schema involved is simply a line or direction with an arrow on it, a vector. To include less as well as more we need a double arrow, and pregnantly an origin or point of reference, like ourselves with a left and a right hand side.

Well-briefed modern boys and girls will recognise this formulation as the y axis of coordinate geometry used for the analysis of algebraic formulations. As such it has nothing whatever directly to do with the line we described initially as distinguishing between "red" and "not-red", the first discrimination of the eye, which we mentioned in passing could be generalised as "x" and "not-x". To point the parallelism which has led to confusion we need to consider the x axis of the coordinate geometry's graph along with the y axis we have just derived. These are all simply different schemas, of which there are potentially an infinite number. In both cases the first term now involves x (a coincidence of the symbolism chosen) and the second "not x" and "minus x" respectively. In spite of the fact that linguistically it appears that the absence of x (not x) can without much loss of rigour be represented as a negative (minus x), in reality an absence and a negative are clean different things. Quite apart from the math, this becomes clear if we try to think what the negative of "red" might be. Perhaps that colour which when combined with red produces white light, negativing (rubbing out) the red? That suggests complementarity rather than opposition.

Moreover, unfortunately there is no such colour, all colour qualities being sui generis and only when all colours (frequencies) are mixed is white light produced. In fact we can not ever see negatives of positives in the real world, only absences, e.g. of light of one group of frequencies or another. Negatives and positives turn out to be simply (mathematical) fictions, without regard to whether the real world provides any fits for them or not. There is no requirement to prove their existential (sc. ontological) status. We don't even need those terms.

There are for sure presumed polarities, for instance in electronics, basically the potential to attract or repulse, in which respect we find atomic and sub-atomic particles marked. But otherwise negative and positive are cultural constructs much favoured by mathematicians and physicists and of great value in calculations and bank accounts. But they are not presented to the eye, not even by a see-saw, they are abstracts, clearly inferred from experience in the phenomenal world but not part of it. They come from shuffling pebbles from one pocket to the other and that sort of thing. They are relative to activities, not to things, coming and going, upwards and downwards, and light and dark for instance. So in the case of electronics, or other subatomic particles schematically opposed, attraction is often regarded as the negative of repulsion, while the absence of attraction is even treated (in semi-conductors a hole in place of a particle for instance) as opposite in value and equivalent to a repulsion. Electrons being negative purely by convention, the travel of an electron through a medium is by convention a flow of negative current. So the similar movement of a hole where an electron (or other negatively charged body) might otherwise be is treated as a positive current. But it is the directions which are opposites (strictly reciprocals) not the electron and its absence. A negative is simply a reciprocal vector.

Nothing here so far is new; at most it is perhaps presented differently.

We can now see further however that the category has hybridised. Neither fish nor fowl it has become a red herring. Originally no more than a boundary which closed, it has acquired an outside and an inside, an exclusion zone as well as a centre, simply because it is an extensive presentation in the mind. There is now, if you can anticipate a little, a continuum across the boundary with the point of origin on it. This is something new and even shocking. It is certainly confusing. Hard pounding! It was not in Hegel's or Marx's books at all.

So now to tie up the relevance to the Dialectic of these two different lines which the mind perceived before speaking – the boundary line or distinction (d!) and the sequential line or criterion/continuum (c!) – perhaps the essential outlines of the Dialectic should first be spelt out, starting with the Hegelian as it was borrowed with insignificant modifications by Marx, and is therefore best known as the Marxian dialectic, as well as being still believed in Europe, and unbelievably even by some presidents and prime ministers. There are of course published critiques of the dialectic, notably that of the late Isaiah Berlin in Britain; but they are literary, even anecdotal, rather than methodological. The methodology really needs by now to be exposed and demolished once and for all, and it is the analysis in terms of c and d which does it.

The Dialectic posits a Thesis (roughly a proposed heading; it is clearly a category, d): a case in point is Feudalism, (a vague and tentative term to describe Norman society, since much revised but still very much in vogue when Victoria was crowned which was not much before when Marx was formulating his dialectical schema for world history). Another more recent application is The Idea of Social and Economic Freedom. Every Thesis is perceived as pregnant with its own doppelganger or opposite, its Antithesis, which arises spontaneously and inevitably from the Thesis, not at all unlike two balloons. The absence of a category is implied by the existence of one (even just the postulation of one when there is a postulated absence to match); while a continuum is conceived as extending infinitely up and down and so with a positive and a negative.

But category and continuum are clean different things – as different as a straight line (the continuum) and a circular one (the category). Put them together nevertheless as if they were one and the same and you get this quaint hermaphrodite feature half one and half the other and capable of populating the world and the brain with a comical coat hanger network, a negative implicit in every positive categorisation, with an ability on top to dream up another category embracing the first two. Examples are Capitalism and Totalitarianism, implicit in and therefore inevitably following upon Feudalism and Social and Economic Freedom respectively. There is plenty of room for interpretation here; there will be parties who prefer different examples and may wish to argue vehemently I have got them all wrong; and it is true I approach their selection quite casually, aware I am on phantom ground. Nevertheless the theory is that it is by the development of Thesis, Antithesis and the third term in the Dialectic, Synthesis, the final realisation resulting from the confrontation and then reconciliation of the Thesis and Antithesis, that both the world progresses and at the same time the mind properly comprehends the process by way of these double repetitive elisions, a double whammy neither of which can stand up to examination.

We are now right inside the dialectical thicket. The thesis is the category initially selected (d') and the antithesis is the implied exclusion category (d'), misprised as a negative. the exclusive property of c' the continuum. The doppelganger not-red arises from the fact every boundary has two sides to it and categorised has a within and a without. The negativity of the dialectic however is superimposed on the mere absence of red outside the category simply by confusion with the other (quite different) line, the continuum, which shows how these two lines have been confused by Hegel and Marx.It is solely this confusion which enables them to invent the dialectical coat hanger pattern supposedly informing both the world historical process (a miasma) and our mental processes (misconceived), both at the same time. The synthesis recognises the common origin of the foregoing two and supposes it is the same as a current commonality, which of course it is not. You can always find another category embracing the two preceding ones. In effect you rub out the two lines you have just drawn in and then draw in another one across the differences between the former two, by means of a quick switch from the category arising from a boundary distinction (d') to a criterion/continuum (c') bridging the boundary.

Perhaps it is the most important single aspect of the Dialectic that it is taken to represent both the way we really think and at the same time the way that world events actually unfold. Because clearly if this is the case once you can grasp and accept the Dialectic methodology your thinking ought from then on to be in line with, synchronised with reality, the way the world goes. You are thinking in objective terms, i.e. the way the objective world proceeds; while everyone else, poor mutts, the subjective thinkers out of kilter with reality, who do not think in dialectical terms, are being suckered. This makes your belief an obstinate one so that you are set to ignore contradictory opinion; and that in turn self-selects for a bigoted ideological mind-set, as well as the wickedest of tyrannies which result. Needless to say my own belief is the whole dialectical gamut is all pie in the sky, and I think I have delineated it as such with my analysis of the confusion of d' and c' The pragmatic view is schemes can be invented galore, much like computer software programmes, for one purpose or another, but hardly to provide every kind of analysis by means of a single programme; and so the dialectic has turned out hopelessly impractical, leading to the most painful political and scientific foul-ups and disillusionments, to say nothing of the human misery of the populations subjected to these wicked ideologies.

The word dialectical itself needs some explanation, being originally from the Greek dia-across and lectos from logos, from legein to read (or choose), that is to say to pick out the meaning of an utterance and so to specify its meaning or import, to read or even to legislate. So the dialect, the way local people talk, is chat but also the logic of speech. I think the speech element is important. It is implicit in dialectic, originally argument and counter argument bandied to and fro as between two folk or perhaps philosophers cross talking in argumentative mood. Then we have to go on to analyse the semantic contents of the term still further: not merely argument and counter argument but prinzip and counter prinzip. Here we access some of the deeper ponderings of the human spirit or psyche. There is first the contrastive consciousness which comes from the very early (even infantile, as described above) perception of the boundary between red and not red for instance, generally x and not-x as fairly exhaustively discussed already above. But then, confusingly, the linear element presents itself alternatively as a continuity at the same time as the discontinuity of the boundary line. The dialectic is caught up in, or perhaps better descends from this confusion of boundary and continuum, a confusion it must be said is still able to fuddle the best of brains and lead to the betrayal of patrimony and even humanity itself. Witness the brilliant buffoon Doctor Fuchs I mentioned above. The gambit goes precisely like this. First of all conceive of a Thesis and Antithesis on either side of a boundary line; pausing to philosophise as much as you wish upon these contrasted categories whatever they may be, praying in aid, wholly improperly, the positive and negative poles of a continuum with a mid-point or point of origin discriminating the two opposite directions. Then comes the Synthesis. Switch about your original point of view entirely now and regard the two elements you have been contrasting as entirely positive and negative aspects of a unifying entity such as a continuum presents. This is your Synthesis. You have as it were stitched up the two elements previously parted, or indeed witnessed their partition and their subsequent overarching unity like a bystander witnessing any other scene change in the everyday world of visual objects. That fixes the whole fandango in the mind. The mind and the world then mirror each other in this dance of the coat hangers, the mental gyrations thus guaranteed to reflect precisely the structured processes of reality. This ideology, a secular neurosis, has probably by now killed more than all the world's old religions put together, because it commands the same certainty in assent as the old religions did but with hundreds of times the power for evil at its disposal due to the progress of technology. It is therefore surely bizarre that dialectical thinking is still admired in certain quarters, and Neo-Darwinist ideology, allowed to refer to any old development at all, is popular, along with particular personal ideologies like Antifa, BLM and Cancel Culture. Each is an ideological miasma, just like the Woke ideology which preceded them.

So it is hard to know whether to dignify Karl Marx with any notice in a chapter on thinking, because when you dismantle the dialectic there is only his outdated Victorian philosophy of the political economy he developed in his 550 pages of Das Kapital in forty years in the British Museum, the taxpayer paying for the heating, in order to outgun the economists. He invented curiosities like Capital, which for him was almost the same as the industrial revolution, not just the initial sum required to set up a business, and surplus value which he extracted from capital to confound the entrepreneur. But he is so much better known and therefore influential than Hegel that his version of the (materialist) dialectical nonsense deserves proper direct attention. He was a perceptive social critic of his day, which was nigh on three hundred years ago now; but his methodology is hopelessly out of date and was always wrong. His dialectic, which he cobbled together from Hegel by (as he put it) standing him on his head, was the blatantly rotten egg in his basket and yet the one beloved by academics for the next century and a half and still admired today even after the communist ideology has failed egregiously everywhere it has been tried. Marx's actual influence has therefore been wholly malign and his intellectual muddles still inform many of the academic establishments around the world. An examination and refutation of the dialectic on scientific and logical grounds is therefore long overdue. Senior wranglers with university tenures have shirked the task or simply failed in it because their thinking never challenged or examined the philosophy involved, I suppose as too difficult to argue much about. The collapse of Marxism has therefore been merely a matter of practicalities and any hostile critique has been based merely on rival social theory, leaving the aficionados still singing famously to their own scores. That is the best you can say.

Hegel's dialectic was a contrast and exchange of liberal prinzips which he believed would be fully realised in practice in due course. Marx's was a contrast and exchange of economic factors which he believed would be realised in political revolution in due course. In both cases Natural Process was involved, informing both the way the world went and at the same time the process of human thinking. It appears to have struck nobody that these coincidental arrangements were a curiosity, as if it were to be expected from the track record of human thinking to date that we would or could naturally keep in step with reality. Any set up which positively entailed any such arrangement of affairs, so blatantly contrary to the human record, ought surely to have been suspect from first formulation. So why not? It was the universal ideological pattern of thinking which was the sole recommendation of Marxism, and that was enough.

There were other curiosities just as bewildering within the philosophy. Economics were apparently naturally determined and their outcomes inevitable, and yet they had to be struggled for bloodily. Nobody asked why they could not just sit back and let Nature take its inevitable course. The true answer was because the whole fabricated scheme was bogus; but nobody realised it, whether they looked forward to the denouement with keen anticipation (well we know Engels did) or regarded it as a threat to their livelihoods. The parties were struggling for and against the inevitable, and comically those against won. But it was a black humour, killing many millions by the way in the name of the dialectic and its winning ways in war.

Marx was a caveman when it came to science. Aristotle must be judged to have known better two thousand years earlier, and he too had one foot in the cave. It was originally Plato's cave in fact, another make-up, but acknowledged as such. Marx's mind-set was of the 1830s, a quarter of a century before Darwin, when Biology was only present as Linnaean Botany, a kind of philately merely. Evolution of the rocks was what Charles Lyell had successfully demonstrated in 1831 in his book "The Principles of Geology", The hard sciences as we now know them, physics, chemistry and of course electronics were barely begun in 1831. Straightforward mechanical forces (Newtonian physics), action and reaction, were the scientific paradigms for the historian and philosopher alike, not a lot different from the thinking of our Stone Age hominid forebears as they flaked their flints hundreds of thousands of years ago. They just lacked its application to the spheres (courtesy of old Isaac Newton).

The human mind is not primarily oriented towards elucidating the truth. It is much more practical than that; which is how we came down from the trees. The mind merely seeks tools for analysing the world, human destiny, reality, call it what you will.

But now a mathematician will tell you the opposite of plus x is minus x. This is where Hegel and Marx messed up. Not x, a ground, is not the same as minus x. X has not been subtracted, it simply is not posited. This is where we need to distinguish a distinction which makes a category from a criterion taken to be a continuum. I don't think the mathematicians had gotten around to this comparison in Hegel's or Marx's day. Frege did not have it.

I believe Bertrand Russell invented the term continuum. We only met once (at undergraduate digs in Oxford) and had to beg to differ (on politics only). He was by then well past his sell by date mentally and involved with the campaign for nuclear disarmament he believed would preserve peace. when in reality of course only the threat of retaliation kept us safe. When falsity beckons ideology falls in line.

Unlike ideology metaphor is a sound methodology, so let us dispose of it. The word metaphor is apparently from the Greek, but actually the etymology (which means the original meaning: as it was first born) goes back a good deal further to the original stone age meanings of the phonemes or original syllables. To have a shot at it: meta-, from mai-ta, which is meaning-become (i.e. development), and then phora from the Greek phorein, which was originally to ejaculate (sexually) and so too it came eventually to mean to project quite generally as well. So metaphor in the context of the development of the meanings of words was to put forward an allied meaning developed from the preceding one as a differently pronounced word; and that is how our million English words got enlarged, and put together, an inter-related texture of meanings developed one from the one before over four hundred thousand years. It has been a game of Chinese whispers over all this time, not just one language but many, jogging along one beside the other. That is not to deny there are also hundreds of minor languages as well, with relatively few speakers and relatively few words which have grown up in jungles and wild places all on their own, probably over a relatively short period of time. Primitive tribes have the bad habit when meeting strangers, of blow piping them first so as not to get one in the eye themselves. I spent eighteen months with the Senoi aborigines in the Malayan jungle in 1955 and 1956, learning their Senoi language – it means "The First People", literally the "first-appearing". They had some three hundred words. They were very friendly. They had blow pipes, but they weren't very good shots. They were pleased to see you and didn't blow pipe you. There was no crime. Everything was shared. They only owned what they wore, men a small bag suspended round their waists woven by their womenfolk, with their "chawat" on they were quite comfortable and would go anywhere, even meet the Duke of Edinburgh, as long as it was in the jungle. Leaving the jungle was a no-no, largely because there were Malays there with firearms. Chawat meant fork, of the branch of a tree, or the crotch of the body, and so the crotch=piece as well (the little bamboo bag). Their words had wide meanings. They had to, as they were so few. Their three hundred had to carry all their thinking, and of course it did limit it quite a bit. My time with them did start me thinking in the linguistic area, sixty seven years ago. I have worked on over a hundred dictionaries since, to study their etymology. Their etymology is how their meanings were first put together.

The ideologies we all know about, Nazism and Communism principally, are assumed to be peculiar philosophies which beguile believers into evil ways. The reality is vastly different, and even more alarming, as an ideology is indeed skewed thinking, and we all adopt an ideology at the drop of a hat, whilst remaining quite unaware we are doing it. An ideology is inward thinking, a single pattern which rejects any thinking which does not fit the ideology. It is wokery, inter-alia. Far from being awake an ideology is a kind of mental sleep walking. You are prevented from recognising the shortcomings of your beliefs because your way of thinking confirms your belief on very little if any independent evidence. You are back in the old stone age tracing the sound ka as the same thing as chipping a flint. You are never going to realise ka is not the same as a flint. Your accepted equivalences to the truth rule. They are the truth.

When you look at the wide spread of "Woke" ideology today in the USA, from President Biden and the Socialist Democratic Party all the way down to Antifa, BLM and Cancel Culture and the plain Marxism behind them all, with even woke media leaders (now supported by a flit Duchess with a belief in white racism whenever it suits), every one of whom appear to be completely unaware that all their thinking is ideological, and indeed ideology has been our common thinking pattern ever since we first spoke, hundreds of thousands of years ago; it is clear there is a bit of catch-up required; and it is the soberer Old World that is going to have to be doing it, because on the other side of the Atlantic pond the ideological thinking has become so overwhelming that the USA has effectively gone mad and taken to rioting and burning and shooting: back to the Wild West with even so-called university professors in California supporting the Antifa/BLM/Cancel Culture/ Woke nest of allied ideologies, which is burning US cities time and time again as I write.

They all come effectively from Marxism and they thus all believe in the dialectic, a ludicrous nonsense which I demolished in my first book on linguistics and I have shown the Dialectic to be simply a mistake, confusing two different straight lines, the boundary and the continuum, which when these different lines are identified the dialectic with its Thesis, Antithesis and Synthesis, all automatically appearing, all automatically disappear again. Mark you this comes after a hundred years of worldwide warfare which has shed more blood than the previous thousand, or maybe even ten thousand years. The figures for comparison are not available. Both Nazism and Communism come equally from Marxism. Don't believe for one moment Nazism is an extreme Right movement. It comes from Nationalistische Arbeiters' Zocialistische Partie, the NAZI Party. So you surely should be thankful for the demolition of the Marxist Dialectic. It is unfortunate the demolition is automatically rejected by all those thinking ideologically - so I have in the next chapter repeated my actual demolition, (only omitting the twenty or so diagrams in the original text, which are not essential, I used them to establish the argument for myself when working it out. But you do have to be aware of the new science of Linguistics and be able to follow an argument. We just have to get the Marxists to understand they can't use the dialectic anymore, because it is demolished; and their abilities for understanding that, where their ideology is contradicted, are somewhat limited. They are dyed in the wool ideologists: they are stuck in their beliefs and can't change, because their ideology won't let them. We have got to get ideology understood for what it is, a pattern of thinking which always involved a misunderstanding, with a history of hundreds of thousands of years. Nobody needs to feel too bad about being taken in by a universal misunderstanding of that age. Every one of us, since we first learned to speak, which is now generally acknowledged to have been at least 400,000 years ago, has been thinking ideologically. It is not only the mistaken philosophy of totalitarian dictators. It is the mistaken ideologies of everyone else as well. Everyone thinks ideologically unfortunately, and always has done. Once you come to understand the nature of ideological thinking you see at once that virtually everything happening today is determined by this mistaken understanding and if we could all of us recognise it and stop allowing our thinking to be skewed by our ideologies the world would be a very different and a much better place. We would be clearing away what can quite legitimately now be described in terms of Hitler's legacy, although he was merely an unthinking practitioner.

It is the universal unconscious ideological thinking which has encouraged, indeed required the bloodshed of the last two hundred years. That is not all. It is this ideological thinking which has made it so difficult for us to abandon any idea once adopted, because ideologies are inward looking and reject anything from outside which does not confirm the current ideology; so that it has slowed down the rate at which we have put together our knowledge of the world, probably by a hundred thousand years, or more, since we first learned to speak and started thinking to any purpose, or very much at all, simply because without speech to tag our thinking as we went along, it was quite hard to keep going and even recover your own thinking after you had thought it. You soon lost your way. So we did not get much thinking done. Ninety nine percent of human thinking has been since we first spoke and could begin to tag what we were thinking with the language we had invented; and to start with, that wasn't much. So this is a challenging book, based on the modern science of Linguistics, which unfortunately is only thinly recognised as yet. How many politicians have ever studied it? What do they know about its relevance to politics? It appears nothing really. They are all without this essential clue to understanding their own thinking.

CHAPTER 2. LINGUISTICS AND THE DEEP HISTORY OF IDEOLOGY

All this extreme leftist ideological thinking, originally from Karl Marx but now described as Woke, as if it were something new, is now subject to review under the terms of this latest branch of science, Linguistics, the study of language as a medium for thought. Up until now ideological thinking has been treated as a semi-insane philosophical peculiarity, a misguided, criminal philosophy which tends to lead to genocide.

But ideology isn't just that, it goes much deeper, and we all suffer from it, and the semi-insanity is there for all of us, yet we are completely unaware of it. What is now known is everyone has always thought ideologically. They haven't all embraced the evil thinking of our recent totalitarian dictators. But humanity has always thought ideologically, ever since we first spoke, and yet has been unaware that this is the case, and still is unaware. In fact language was our first ideology and that is why it still is. The whole story of our formation of language is relevant to understanding this, and how we were able to agree on their meanings as we learned to utter our first phonemes, one after the other. It could be Ba was the first phoneme we said, the phoneme most easily produced, all you have to do is to part your lips with a slight puff. My first grand-daughter, before speaking, with a toy telephone from her elder brother, put it to her ear and said "Ba". Her mother, who had just had a lecture from me that Ba meant "Lips speaking" in the Stone Age because to all agree on the meanings of the phonemes as we learned to utter each in turn we adopted a meaning in each case of an echoic sound in nature; but as we could find no Ba sound in nature decided it must mean lips speaking, nearly fell off her chair. However thinking how to get everyone with the same meaning for each sound as we learned to utter each phoneme, (syllable), was a difficulty and may have taken us quite a time to get it understood. (Perhaps a thousand years. Who knows?) Four hundred thousand years ago, what did sounds (phonemes, single syllables) mean? Without any speech, we invented a way of establishing agreed meanings for the three original vowels and twenty-three consonantal stop phonemes. This is what established the universal ideological thinking. So how we did it must now be spelt out in detail if we are going to grasp how and why human thinking has inevitably fallen into these ideological patterns ever since, which is now powering up these modern ideologies, mostly copying Karl Marx. They don't have to be Nazi or Communist ideologies but they do always carry some of their absurdities. I have shamelessly borrowed from my Linguistics books to cover what I call this deep history of language (and the thinking which goes with it) in this chapter. It challenges the ill-informed, those who have generally ignored this most recent science, Linguistics, which deals with etymology, a term originally Greek and means the study of how the phonology is originally related to the semantics, how words have come to mean what they do.

It results in a serious audit of how we think, and that in turn reveals the pattern of ideology which we have all been inclined to follow for the last four hundred thousand years, yet without being aware of it. But then you do not naturally think how it is you are thinking while you are actually doing it, and the sequence of your thinking suggests that is its justification. We are already getting into the pattern of ideology.

I think it can be said those who are unaware of the ideological discoveries of Linguistics are quite simply ill informed, and need to brush up their thinking, which otherwise will be taken up with the ideologies which currently are sweeping the United States and making fools of very many people, as well as burning cities and threatening other people.

Phonemes are just single (stop or consonantal) sounds, but they all need a vowel phoneme with them so they can be pronounced; and three vowels were first recognised, a, i and u, (aaa, eee and ooo). So how was it that we did agree meanings? I only know one possible way. If by any chance you think you can think of another, do drop me a line. I have been thinking my way since 2006 in print! Much of the Linguistics you will come across today, for instance in the British Open University, is only applied linguistics, often courses for seriously autistic folk to get them to read and write, or to qualify teachers so they can teach them to do it. That has nothing to do with the recent discoveries of the science, of which apparently the Open University knows nothing.

It was by echoism, a relationship between one sound and another, one in speech the other in nature that we were able to solve the problem. But it had to be imaginative echoism because precise echoism was not to be found. We thought the various sounds we recognised in nature would or could be represented by those phonemes most appropriate for them in speech. But of course we were addressing the relationships the other way around: we all identified the meanings of the single phonemes as we learned to utter them by what they appeared to be echoic of in nature. That was the trick which got us all thinking of the same meanings for the sounds as we learned to utter them. It was a fanciful exercise, no doubt aided by a lot of pointing and reiterating the phoneme, slowly gaining supporters, but it did get us all thinking the phonemes each meant the same for all of us. With no speech to debate the matter this was no mean achievement. It won't have been apparent to our bare bottomed forebears in their naming committees outside their caves all on day one, pictured on the covers of my books, the origin of our civilisation today. For all we know it may have taken a thousand years, but anyway we did it, else we could not have learned to use language to communicate. This is ultimately what the science of linguistics is about. It's study is etymology, the original meanings given to words (by way of the original supposed meanings of the individual constituent meaningful phonemes, now our meaningless letters of the alphabet retained just so we can spell our words.

Linguistics was not, when I first wrote acknowledged as a science because it dealt with language, a human activity. Scientific American, a few years later, were carrying articles announcing the new science. However for half a century Professor Chomsky of Massachusetts Institute of Technology, an American university, has held linguistics in thrall with his philosophical "transformational grammar" which he originally believed to have been, at least in part, prompted by our genes. I dare say he had the same problem as I did over how folk all got to thinking of the same meanings; and did not think of the fanciful echoic route. (Or perhaps he didn't think about it at all). He was still only a student when he dreamed up his transformational grammar. But, as Linguistic science now puts it, our legs are determined by our genes, but not the Sunday walks we may take, and similarly our brains are determined by our genes, but not the thoughts we may think. It is what philosophers know as a category error. Legs and brains are physical phenomena but walks and talks are their activities. Indeed it has left the grammarians with a mind, supposedly a phenomenon, with nowhere specific to locate it, when it is actually an abstract term to describe all of our thinking and is not a thing of any kind and therefore can not be located, any more than grammar can be, which is a relatively late addition to our linguistic thinking, as is algebra also and symbolic logic. Traditionally the mind has been regarded as a sort of phenomenal doppelganger of the brain, which it is not; and the latter researched to see where our ideas fit in; but they can not be fitted in, any more than walking can be fitted in our legs. We could not think without our brains any more than we could walk without our legs. It is that simple! The relationship of electrical activity in our brains and mental (thinking) activity is completely unknown and may well remain so for ever, anyway so long as we only have the brains we currently have. It is argued our sight can be traced in the brain. But it is not the vision we experience which is traced but merely the physicality. We should not go looking for where a picture is located anywhere behind the eyes in the head.

So to return to how we got everyone thinking of the same meanings of the phonemes as we learned to utter them, I estimate the sharpest phoneme we uttered, which was taken to be Ka, was therefore taken to represent the sharpest sound in nature, which was the chipping of flints, the sound of flint striking flint. It may not sound much, but it was a remarkable achievement to invent the same meanings which could be grasped by everyone, so we could acquire a common language. In my linguistics books I have a chapter on each phoneme and how it got its meaning(s). I just list the conclusions below. I am not repeating the previous 1600 pages here.

They could not find the Ba sound in nature. Can you? Sheep say Ma'a not Ba'a. So to get language together they said it must be the lips themselves speaking, so it meant lips speaking, and lips are the fleshy bits, so Ba also meant flesh, and then the unvoiced thinned version of Ba, which is Pa, meant the thinned version of flesh which is skin, and so on - and on and on. However long it was before we had enough to make much use of it, however long it took, eventually we got it all together. Else we would not now be speaking. We invented language, and the thinking which went with it. That is the point, and it was ideological thinking. Linguistics is the science of language, including our original ideology, and how it has developed. It has been a human whimsey from the start. We have made it all up as we went along. There has been no process, evolution, like with Charles Darwin's single (ideological) origin of biological species, an ideological evolution which has since been borrowed for pretty well any development at all, and must now be specifically dismissed for the activity of speaking. In fact evolution has been taken over for general use for any process which is identified, even for car design which has little in common with procreation and the survival of the fittest in an (evanescent) environment. Even that is now modified by the discovery of viral inter-species genetic changes and not just from sexual procreation as Charles Darwin imagined. (However I guess viral evolution, although undeniable, has been rather modest, and in no way discredits Darwin's achievement). The viral evolution is in David Quammen's book, "The Tangled Tree" of 2018.

I am now going to put down the phonemes that we learned to utter and their meanings which I believe we agreed to give them, which became established. I don't suppose I have it all absolutely correct, but the overall pattern is right.

You can immediately see with more than one phoneme it would be possible to improve on meanings by adding meanings together - indeed in due course, whole strings of them in fact, which is how we got to have words, after any number of thousands of years of speaking. The first adoption of independent words as meaningful nuggets of sounds is recorded in the Akkadian (Jewish) Bible, as the Tower of Babel, only some five thousand years ago, after some 395 thousand years at least nominally still as strings of meaningful phonemes, when God "confounded" original language, and words became independent and no longer composed of strings of constituent meaningful original phonemes. They were still pronounced the same but their make up was no longer remembered, words were now just single nuggets of meaning. However the Biblical record is total confusion too, it was early days, thinking was still remarkably primitive compared with today. There wasn't actually any Tower, nor any Babel. What there was was a Tau of Bab El in Sumerian language The Tau was a ta-u or second birth (i.e. a Change), and it was a change of Bab El, and Bab El was the Mouth of The Lord (i.e. God's original language), in other words there was a change in the original ordering of language. God's ordering of course was just the original pattern for which it was assumed He was directly responsible, since by then the way it had been done was forgotten.

Whereas up until then language had still been composed, at least nominally, of individual meaningful phonemes which were used in strings to make 'words' to derive an extended set of meanings, and how this had been done had to be recollected, at least nominally, every time the string was strung once more to use as a word. But now, with the Tau of Bab El, the Change of the Original Language Pattern, you only had to remember the meaning of the string of sounds, or word, not bothering any more with the intermediate meanings of the phonemes. Indeed it turned out you did not need the constituent meanings as originally strung any more at all, and now nobody knows what they were - which left me having to guess them. We just have the letters which still tell us the pronunciations.

Before the Tau of Bab El, the meaningful strings of phonemes which were used to make up "words" had to be remembered, at least in theory. The fact is as long as the strings were remembered along with the composite meanings of the words, it was less important exactly how the string was composed. A string might not actually convey by itself the meaning it was supposed to convey. But the meaning might nevertheless be known from general agreement. Language took off, because meanings established themselves, regardless whether the sounds of the words were well put together or not. No doubt some were and some weren't. To start most were, and finally most weren't, because by then they were otiose even before the Tower of Babel was recognised and declared, I believe in Sumerian first as the Akkadian tribe, the first known Semitic tribe, who wrote the Bible, were at that time goat-herds, and learned much of their stuff from the Sumerians. They even borrowed the whole of their first chapter, Genesis, from the Sumerians - an earlier copy in Sumerian has now been found - because it was judged to be scientific and so good. That was how the Tau of Bab El got changed to Tower of Babel. It was a mistranslation of the Sumerian.

When we started out with individual phonemes and were allocating meanings for each of them the initial meanings were problematic: how to get everyone to think the same. A language which meant different things for different people was not a very useful one. It was essential the meanings should be uniform, the same for everyone, and this first picking was critical. There needed to be some guiding principle directing the meanings, which got everyone thinking the same; and you must remember that at this stage by definition, we had no language and could not discuss the matter at all. We could only squark and gesture. How on earth could we have done it? There wasn't really any clear-cut guiding principle. Echoism was the nearest approximation to a principle. That is all you can say. Meaning was allocated from appropriate agreed similitude. So the phoneme which was our sharpest sound (ka) had a natural meaning for a sound in nature which was sharpest, and this was supposed to be the sound of striking flint on flint, which had been going on for a million years. The phoneme Ka meant the sound of a flint struck. All the others acquired meanings in the same rough manner, I guess from this first orienting one, but it might have been from Ba which was identified as the sound of the lips, because there is no obvious ba sound in nature. Sheep say ma'a not ba'a. I have had a go at working them all out. It took me more than twenty years. You can get sort of hooked up

71

with the pastime, with your ideological thinking of course. I am not suggesting I thought of nothing else because of course I did. But it took me about twenty years. Most of the time I was retired however so I did have quite a bit more time than I had before for thinking about the deep history of language. It doesn't even matter all that much how right I was and am. What is needed is the realisation of what had to be done in order to get us up and thinking and speaking. You aren't going to understand it by not thinking about any of it, which is the usual posture. It just happens to introduce you to the universal ideology involved in language at the same time. Language was our first ideology.

Here are the meanings which appear to have originally got taken to be the meanings. The phonemes (sounds) are the letters today. They no longer have any meanings. They just have the sounds of the original phonemes, without any meanings for making up the meanings of words any more. We use them for spelling the sounds and the meanings of the words are now quite separate, at any rate as far as our conscious minds are concerned. Witchcraft's words of power suggest you might be able to trawl up some deep history from the subconscious but we don't need to bother with any of that here. I just want to pop in here that to imagine that in some magic manner we developed human language is obviously just wrong. It all had to be worked out, and amazingly it was. It is surely probable it took some time. We have no way of estimating how long it took. I am not sure that it matters any more now either. There has been ample time since we first spoke. It was we who made all these meanings up. Who else? I just follow the alphabetical sequence of the sounds. Why not?

Ba   The labial, the sound of lip on lip: mouth, flesh on flesh, flesh, muscle, fleshing out, burgeoning, the binary body, binary symmetry, the biosphere, being, the haunch (another fleshy bit), to leg it and go, to be fleshed (i.e. alive), and so to be, and so on. No sound outside in nature you see. Sheep say ma'a, not ba'a, sheep are described as mouthing, like God.

Ka   The sound of flint on flint, strike, flake, break apart, shape, make, kindle, force, hard, sharp, rock, driving force, drive, life force, male soul, rock, land, place.

Da   An expansion of Ta, birth, become, pass across, do, give effect, reveal, disclose, give, and so on. (this will have been over the years, not all at once)

Fa   A powerful puff, as for firing a dart from a blow pipe for instance. An approximation of Ba. A dialectical elision of Pa and Ha (one of the naughty bits), the Pahai or orgasmic piece, the male genitalia, and so on and so on. Fa-ka to make with the orgasmic piece, (the first explanation of the derivation shock, of the four letter F word in English).

Ga   A voiced expansion of Ka (q.v.), impetus, go, and so on.

Ha   A gasp, hot, hurt, hideous, harm, harry, horror, haunt, hilarity, hedonism, any sudden sensation, delight, ecstasy, orgasm, hooray, hi, joy, rejoicing and so on. Originally any sharp sense, what the mugg said who picked up a white hot stone to throw back into the hearth thinking it was wood, as he felt the burn, whence any traumatic sensation, even humour. (Over the years)

La   With a curling tongue, nasty taste, brackish liquid, the instinct of liquids (water) to slope down, go flat and become brackish as it goes downwards, slope, slip, slide, lean, ladder, flat, loose, flow, lye, salt water, the ocean, skyline at sea, and so both line and circle, loop, orbit, the sun (orbiter), luminescence, light, and so on. (Over the years)

Ma   Stress, hungry, mother, milk, liquid, water, eat, meat, the paired (dialectically opposite) sound with ish, because they are the only two continuous stops, all the others can not be extended, hissing and humming: heavy, go down, dead, kill, harm, mass, massive, earth, to earth, to plant, to impregnate, germinate (seeds), gestate, and so on. (Over the years) Ish was fire because when you dipped your burning brand, to keep off the sabre toothed tigers at night, in a puddle at dawn it said Ish.

Na   The sound made letting out the breath after holding it – from excitement or anticipation, or both (another naughty bit): from on orgasm, so ejaculate, push, protrude, exhibit, present, the presented, the present (now), show, profess, explicate, expositor, prophet; also present, gape, round out, open, empty, null, nil, no, nice, and so on. Nabi Issus, Prophet Jesus, nabi, (from na-bai) explicator bum, roaming prophet.

Pa   A spit or a puff. The thinned diminutive of Ba, flesh and so skin, small or thin piece of flesh or foliage, skin, shoot, penis, piece, surface, roof, visible surface, patch, lid, rim, the ostensive, 'the' in Ancient

Egyptian, and Sanskrit (5 pages of meanings for pa), and so on.

Ra   A rapid rattling repetitive sound, the tongue going back and forth almost with the speed of light, repetition, reflex action, light ray (radar style, there and back), ray, rayed, sun, eye, see, seen, colour, straight, elongated, sun rayed, growing, played upon, raise, rise, rouse, engorged, ripe, lots of rises, rough, ruffled, and so on.

Ish   The sound of a burning brand (to repel predators at night) extinguished in a puddle at dawn (ishshsh). Fire, bright, light (shine), shone on, visible, see, the instinct of the flame for going up, up, vertical, a drawn vertical stroke, one, light (weightless, no ma, the pair of oppositional continuous stops, hissing and humming), hot, warm, comfortable, pleasant, ease, animal (warm blooded, with ish), animal marker, brer, mobile, activity, alive, life, lively, active, and so on.

Ta   The staccato sound or crack of a breaking branch (for firewood), as opposed to Ka, the clink of flint on flint when knapping flints. To break, to break in two, to cut in two, to divide in two, two, a cut or slit, the birth canal, vagina, parturition, to become two, to give birth, to be born, birth, a coming into being, a becoming, a happening, a natural event as opposed to an agential act, a ray source (from the sun, originally a world vagina birthing light into the world each day), a source, and so on.

Wa Shivering, cold, wet, water, fear, and so on. Much later an easement of the glottal stop.

Vowels – in early speech the vowels were only three: A (aaa), I (eee), and U (ooo). Together the a and i. made e and a and u made o, later.

- A is the middle general easy vowel and ranks first as the exemplar of continuous unmodulated vowel tones, extension spatial or temporal, ongoing, going, ever, away, omnipresent, eternal, etc; but also as vacuous and empty, air, absence of a quality or structure as with water or air.

- I is the thinned diminutive reduplicative vowel, micro, -ing, -ed, plural, itemisation, it, which, he, I, and so on.

- U is the dual, inclusive, completive, substantive vowel, rounded out, "all done gone finish", "sab khatm ho gaya" in Hindi, dialectically embracing the other two vowels, all of them, both of them, and so on.

The whole human lexicon derives from these simples; though that is not to say that nothing has been added, or that other practices are not in evidence today. I have embarked on the derivation of meanings from each elementary Lithic phoneme in the 'psychosomatic trees' in my books on linguistics, with an individual chapter on each of the phonemes, and I do not think you are going to pick up all the above just from this listing, with meanings cascading from each other like the phenotypes in a family tree. So why not just accept that these phonemes, or at least something like them, came to be thought good, without going through all the reasoning. In any case it goes back hundreds of thousands of years. We just need to bear in mind that it happened, and the ideology of language was in it.

What is important is to understand we made all this up ourselves, it did not come from anywhere else.

Bertrand Russell identified the continuum, a line which should NOT be treated as the same as the original common old boundary line. One thing is that with a boundary line you are effectively looking across it, but with a continuum you are effectively looking up and down it. Russell never went on to pick the Marxist dialectic to pieces, he was past his sell-by date, and the fact is everyone else's commentaries so far on the dialectic have just been chat, objecting to it on moral and or political grounds, because of the sadistic genocides it has introduced – which is all very well, but it counts for nothing if you are politically in favour of the Marxist revolutionary ideology. Marxists don't bother with chat. As classic ideologists they know they must be right, and naturally reject as false, as a matter of simple logic, anything which is not consonant with their own ideological beliefs, because if it is not consonant it must be wrong. The ideology is unchallengeable. All ideological thinking is solely inward looking and thus self confirming. Of course all scientific thinking is ideological thinking, and unless it is carefully and consciously edited – which quite often it is not – it can confuse scientific thinking so that new knowledge is held back. I am acutely conscious of this. I am not a professor and no professor will read my books because if it is not in the scientific establishment it is not scientific and should not be bothered with. Every ideology automatically holds back escape from it, it is inward looking and self confirmatory. If you are committed to a system of belief that silly, it is I suppose no wonder that it fails to be recognised. The psychological penalty is too extreme. Anyhow, that is how it is. No ideologist will recognise his ideology as illusory. So it inevitably involves some degree of psychological disintegration. So it is necessary to broadcast the universal psychological pattern of ideological thinking so people are forewarned, and do not embark on the Hitler Path. It would be quite nice too if it was recognised those who profess science don't know everything and their beliefs will not all be right.

However I have demolished the (Marxist) dialectic once and for all, showing the pattern to be simply the result of the confusion of the two different straight lines, the boundary and the continuum. Marx was a caveman when it came to science, and he is, of course, at the same time, the classic ideologist, with the two most blood-stained modern totalitarianisms, Nazism and Communism, springing directly from his ideology.

China of course hosts too perhaps the most all-pervading ideological self possession of all time, which already with Chairman Mao was responsible for massive genocidal starvation which he said he did not believe even when he could see it in front of his own eyes. There is the most extraordinary and revelatory book written by Mao's Chinese personal (western educated) doctor, and single (only) friend of twenty two years, from 1949 to Mao's death in 1966, who fled China when he found, after Mao had died, the politburo planned to kill him because if left alive he might contradict them if they wanted to make up a different version of history at any time, which is of course done whenever political circumstances require it. Safely in America, relatively safe anyway, he decided to shed his total subservience to Mao's every whim, all of it mere fabrication, which he had knowingly endured for twenty two years, it is hard to know why, but there is no doubt he was originally a believer but 22 years confronting the insanity of it all cured him entirely; and in retrospect he says he can't make out why himself. Initially it was of course because he believed in the Communist, Marxist philosophy and mission to set the world to rights, but he came to realise that was entirely false and even absurd, in view of Mao's insane behaviour, sometimes staying in bed for days, at others uttering flurries of instructions, often quite impractical. But somehow he went on as if he actually accepted Mao's insanity. He was locked into his thinking, still under the ideological illusion. But now he had decided to come clean on Mao as he actually was, the complete unthinking ideologist for whom his personal fancies were the only reality and everything else was false, even when he was looking at it. There was no starvation when he could see the people starving in front of his own eyes, and Dr. Zhisui Li could see them with him. Now this of course would rank as insanity, which it is not good to have in a dictator with totalitarian authority over a country and controlling everything people may do or think. To be ruthlessly honest it is not much better in a flit princess by marriage who also believes, with the 1930s German Socialist philosopher Herbert Marcuse, that as there actually is no objective reality at all after all, each individual can make up their own truth, and believe whatever it is they like to believe as their truth; and everyone else is doing the same. She appears to have picked up this absurdity from Antifa in California since she has no education herself other than from Hollywood, and it was Antifa that dug Marcuse out long after he had been contradicted and ridiculed by Wittgenstein who said in contradiction "the world is what it is and not another thing". Marcuse was a German Socialist, a mad Marxist who had the dialectic churning out for him his personal made up truths. Some of President Joe Biden's Socialist Democratic Party also enjoy the ideologies of Antifa, BLM, and Cancel Culture along with their underlying Marxism, complete with materialist dialectic. These are all classic ideologies. They mostly use Marx's reputation to bolster their beliefs. But he made it all up in the first place. He did not claim to be an economist. He regarded economists (financiers) as class enemies. The economy he made up was a political economy, just a philosophical fancy to defeat his class enemies and his theories of value which were used to demonstrate the employer was stealing "surplus value" from the worker. If the entrepreneur was not paying his workers a fair wage it still did not make any sense of surplus value which was a mix of capital, materials and labour, not one of which was a sufficiently stable entity to be treated as a fixed value; and the mix was a gibberish. The value of manufactured goods of all kinds is now recognised as a measure of the market - which of course depends upon numerous circumstantial conditions, none of them able to be fitted in with

Marx's Capital, materials (commodities) and value. His forty years in the British museum, when he was largely dependent upon the business Communist Engels to advise him of conditions in British factories, was quite frankly a pernicious fabrication and it would have been better if he had never thought to set up a philosophy of political economy copying Hegel's philosophy, the German eighteenth century idealist philosopher, although not because he promoted socialism but because he directed it all in the wrong direction, trying to use the dissatisfaction of the workers to incite a revolution in order to kill off everyone except the workers. This was in any case overly ambitious, as can now be seen. It was in fact based on the ridiculous assumption aristocrats could only think aristocratic thoughts, middle class citizens could only think middle class thoughts and workers could only think working class thoughts; and it was only the working class who had no property to defend, [well actually just not much, but they clung to it] so they were the only honest thinkers, and that was why a social revolution was required in order to kill off all the incurable dishonest thinkers. If this is not actually insanity it is something very much like it. There is no evidence whatever the brains of social classes are different. Indeed the opposite is true. We all start out with virtually identical mental capacities. Whether we finish up as Einstein or Hitler or just a worker is a matter of subsequent circumstances. Intelligence is an additional skill, largely built later.

The world was not at that time engaged in fraudulence to the extent that it is now, after Marx had provided the (insane) key incentive for everyone to surrender to their ideological thinking, abandoning reality for their preferred beliefs.

In Das Kapital he acknowledges England was well ahead of Germany during the industrial revolution. And he made clear he was describing factory conditions in England so the Germans could learn what their future would be – except that the British had passed Factory Acts to limit the predation of the British employers, which Germany had not; and if they now still did not in a few years introduce similar legislation the conditions in German factories would be even worse than those in England as he wrote. He had been building in these warnings over the forty years in the British Museum, (at least eight years in gaps due to sickness). For much of the time sitting down to write and not washing he had boils on his bottom which in no way improved his perception of social conditions in England. Perhaps if the British Museum chairs had been designed for the long term sedentary with softer cushions we might have had less revolution.

Meanwhile, the classic book on Mao Tse Dung is by Dr. Zhisui Li, "The Private Life of Chairman Mao", 682 pages, republished in paperback by Arrow Press in 1994, described by the Regius Professor Oxford historian, Hugh Trevor-Roper, later Lord Dacre, as "a classic... I

see Dr Li as the Tacitus of modern China".
Trevor- Roper's judgment wasn't always 100%.
He identified some forgeries as Hitler's diaries.
The book by Dr. Li has many photographs too.
But its main import is the horrific delineation of
the impact of ideological thinking on the human
mind. It should therefore really be read by
everyone with any pretensions of understanding
political matters and the effects of the universal
ideological thinking of mankind for the last four
hundred thousand years. We are not going to rid
ourselves of this wrong thinking until many
more of us understand what is involved. We
have to accept we have all, each one of us, been
in thrall to ideology for 400,000 years, and we
can not guard against its many mischiefs until
the effect of ideology is widely understood.
Now you can see why I have titled the book
"Universal Ideology Exposed". Ideology is built
into language, which was our first ideology. We
have lost trace of that first language, but I have
re-identified it with its inbuilt ideology in my
study of scientific linguistics.

Anyone understanding the universal
ideological thinking by all of us ever since we
spoke 400,000 years ago should be aware all
ideologies are fraudulent and should not be
believed by anyone with any understanding. But
there are not many with any understanding of
human thinking today. That is why the world is so
largely astray. The nineteenth, twentieth and
twenty first centuries are the Malevolent Years for

which Karl Marx is responsible because of his absurd ideological compositions, in spite of the enormous improvements in living conditions, health, wealth, science and pretty well everything else, including civilisation, due to the industrial revolution, which this silly little man has garbled up.

It is not that we have suddenly all got nastier, but it is true we have all got more ideological. Napoleon was the first fighter in Europe locked in to ideology entirely. It destroyed him. He was the first Fascist. His ideology was quite simple, he was just a corporal to start with. He decided France was the central power in Europe and so the country was destined to rule the continent, if it had the Will to Rule and was prepared to seize control by force of arms. All the rest in the subsequent European nest of Fascist ideologies (Germany, Italy, Spain, France, Portugal) got their ideological thinking from him, one after the other, including his militarism too. They latched on to the ideology, as to the manner born. Well they were. The fact is we all are, it is just for the most part we don't know it. Most of us know we don't know everything and so don't trust our inclination to think ideologically as if we did. It is only all those who decide to have it their way who do, and that is an increasing body of humanity these days, partly at least because information technology gives us access to so much more information that many more of us think we are sufficiently kitted out to make out a scheme which can be ideologically validated. I suppose this can be associated with the perception which has acquired the designation of Woke. These woke folk have come to the conclusion they can see the reality so much more clearly that it is as if they have awoken from a predecessing ignorant sleep.

Nothing could be further from the truth. They have actually fallen completely into the ideological dream world which has already plagued humanity for four hundred thousand years. Professors and universities who have grown used to thinking in accordance with their own scientific ideologies find it easy to adopt further similar ideological thinking with markedly less justification. It is nevertheless astonishing to hear professors in universities in California have actually joined Antifa, a Marxist ideology, no doubt still following the absurd Marxist dialectic which I have demolished, copied from my original 2006 book. Antifa has a totalitarian ideology exposed by Dr. Andy Ngo in his 2021 book "Unmasked" in the USA. Antifa thought they had succeeded in killing him by hitting him on the head with an iron bar and then trampling on him in the street, as soon as they recognised him as a critic. A critic of an ideology is quite properly killed by the ideologists. To challenge an ideology is a capital offence. Dr. Ngo is a Vietnamese American journalist, after his parents fled to the USA when they could endure the tyranny of the Communist (Marxist) ideology no longer, when he was still a boy. But after six months in hospital his brain and other injuries were fully recovered; and with incredible bravery he masked himself up and joined them to expose their Nazi ideology by learning it all from their propaganda on riots in the streets of many American cities, and published it all in a book "Unmasked". It is sobering to find Hitler's legacy of totalitarian thinking well established in American universities. Adolescent students are peculiarly liable to fall for ideological thinking, because they do not have any established intellectual track record of their own thinking. It is universal ideological thinking which must be unmasked. Ideologists generally lose, after much bloodshed, because their thinking is fraudulent and lets them down. Even the European Union is in origin another Nazi plot from 1950, and the European political constitution was written by Dr. Goebbels in 1943, when Nazism was at its zenith, for Hitler's post war "Thousand Year European Fourth Reich". It was copied by the German war criminals imprisoned by the International Court at Nuremberg when the USA let them all out again and hijacked the meeting of the tripartite International Study Group on Germany, (France, Britain and USA) convened in 1951 to revise the Occupation Statutes for the Allied Occupation Zones, in the Foreign Office in London, (for which I was the Secretary General and took all the minutes for weeks, getting a hundred copies of them typed every night on a bank of Gestetner machines in the attic of the Foreign Office in King

Charles Street, opposite Downing Street, the first copy going hot foot in a locked red box to Prime Minister Clem Attlee, who when it was all done was good enough to thank me before I had resigned in disgust. In my digs I had been having cold suppers out of the fridge, homing by taxi as the tubes were closed.

Information technology has certainly given us access to a far wider span of information, so that our intellectual energies can be devoted to building our ideologies instead, and we have simply become more argumentative, our ideological thinking teaching us we must be right. It is what ideologies do to you. Most people still think an ideology is just a wicked philosophy which disturbs the judgment of criminal psychopaths like Hitler and Stalin. That is indeed what ideologies do do; but it is also the common thinking pattern of Sapiens Sapiens ever since we first learned to speak. That must surely need thinking about. We may not all be potential Hitlers but we are with absolute certainty all potential ideologists, which gives us the potential for unthinking radicalism and lack of scruple, together with a self-belief which is astonishing, a refusal to consider any reservation at all. An ideology can lead to autism. Those with an autistic leaning will jump into bed with an ideology because it validates their self-belief. Unfortunately, the rest of us are not far behind them.

When I published my first book on Linguistics, academia, the professors in the universities, believed we had first spoken only forty thousand years ago, which of course meant they effectively thought we had progressed some ten times as fast as we actually had, getting from first speaking to our present state of knowledge and science in forty thousand years in place of four hundred thousand. The stretches of time involved in human development had quite simply not begun to be seriously addressed. However I think the four hundred thousand years they have now reached already will do. It is such a long period of time it is virtually incomprehensible.

We really must now address the issue and put in place some understanding of reality and of the effect of the universal ideological thinking which is pulling the world to pieces with diversive ideologies, which develop like mental cancers and make people think like zombies, so the world is reduced to a world of universal squabblers about virtually everything. US presidents, along with statesmen around the world, are slaves of ideology, and slavery guilt is the ideology of America. We have had Winston Churchill painted as a believer in slavery. If that isn't insanity I don't know what is. He was born in the nineteenth century. Quite apart from anything else he was too late. The British had destroyed the trade before he was born, capturing over two hundred slaving ships, most of them Arab boats on the East coast of Sub Saharan Africa, as well as of course the smaller number of boats slave trading with America. The owners of slaves were Arabs and colonialists in America and the Caribbean.

All language is a single texture, every word related to every other, mostly remotely, when you work backwards to show the way our thinking has come forwards; so there is a thread from human thinking which can prove black is white, that whiteness is evil, anything you like; but sanity does not believe a word of it, only ideology does. With these extreme beliefs supported by ideological thinking you show yourself to be an ideologist, and so should be disregarded. Ideological beliefs are floating in a void, lodged in the human head. They are not the reality. There is an obvious reality which enables us to distinguish fancy from reality. Over fifty years ago Herbert Marcuse, an absurd German Socialist philosopher in the 1930s, contemporary with Hitler's National Socialism, who believed there was no objective reality so everyone could make their own truth, who was contradicted by a far superior thinker, the Austrian born Cambridge philosopher Wittgenstein who said "The world is what it is and not another thing". You can make up what you like, but it should not be believed unless it happens to be the case. The woke is not the case, merely an illusion believed by ideological thinkers. It enables them to believe what they want. But the posture is not evidential, merely ideological. It provides no evidence, it is a change of tack from normal thinking to ideology.

So this is a short book to knock the stuffing out of ideology by establishing the subconscious universality of the ideological thinking of humankind ever since we first spoke. Over that time I guess it has set us back a hundred and fifty thousand years, or more, which must seem unbelievable. But it is just in the last 250 years that it has killed anything like so many people, with the fighting started by Napoleon Buonaparte, prompted I suppose by the violence of the French Revolution, acting upon the universal common ideological commitment of all Napoleon's thinking. He was the first Fascist in the European nest of them; all the rest come, directly or indirectly, from him. Now in the twenty first century we see ideologies raining down on us from all around the world. Examination and recognition of this specialty in all our thinking, ever since we first spoke, is thus long overdue. Of course all science and religions involve ideological thinking too, so we can't do without them; but then again we can't do with them either, without proper understanding of the shortcomings of the thinking.

You can see most of scientific advance has been in these last few decades, and virtually all of it in the last two centuries; but the evil political ideological thinking has rendered the world heinous for the last few generations. Marx first composed his ideological fabrication in his head in the 1820s, (Das Kapital later) before much of modern science. When I wrote my first book on Linguistics, the most recent science, already recognizing the techniques of linguistics demonstrated the universal ideological thinking of all humanity, I had realised already it came from far back.

Now thinking to write on ideologies specifically, and highlight the evil and the universality of this mode of thinking, I thought of Karl Marx and his books and bought both The Communist Manifesto and Das Kapital (in English translation) and set about them, as I decided to expose them as setting out the classic political ideology, fathering both Nazism and Communism. Marx, and Georg Hegel in the previous century, had invented, (well re-invented, it was an illusion somehow dug out of the prehistoric mind), the dialectic. The Ancient Egyptians appear to have had their vowels in a dialectical pattern already, perhaps seven millennia back. There is no earlier record. The Sumerian language is barely got together yet, but it appears to have been spoken before the last Ice Age melted, as long ago as 10,000 years before the present, the time when the Oceans rose 160 feet and flooded Eastern Malaya, (mistranslated in the Jewish Holy Bible from the Sumerian as the Garden of Eden), which as a result is now the South China Sea; and the Adamites (Noah is sailors in Sumerian) sailed from eastern Malaya, as the sea rose, to Mesopotamia to rebuild their cities there, only to be shortly captured by the Akkadians who borrowed the Sumerian Chapter of Genesis for their Bible because they thought it so good. So Noah's flood was inadvertently transferred in their book to their own original homeland in the highlands above Mesopotamia around Lake Van, instead of eastern Malaya. Lake Van of course was always an impossibility.

The South China Sea is now recognised as the historical reality as the location of Noah's flood, which drove the Adamites out of their homeland. The Gates of Hercules (Gibraltar) let the Atlantic into the Mediterranean basin at the same time, and then into the Black Sea. We do not know how much water was in the Mediterranean basin before the melt, quite likely only a relative puddle or two. Any inhabitants in the basin may have had to run for the shore or the current islands, but we haven't heard about it because there was no Akkadian Jewish tribe writing a Bible in the Mediterranean at the time.

I doubt if there are many alive today who have actually read any of either The Communist Manifesto or Das Kapital, in English Translation, and fewer still in the original German. I had read neither, but have now some, but not all of either. You could not have a more idiotic and absurd example of an ideology even if you set out to try and make one up like Mao Tse Dung. The original absurdities are all by now laid bare. On the other side of the pond today, in the United States of America, ideologies are running riot. This little squib I am putting together is intended to show them up for the non-sense that they are, a relic of the Wild West culture of two hundred years ago, never really fully abandoned in the two hundred years to date, and now, alas, again in full flower, with intellectual and political understanding sadly diminished. It is said there are woke university professors in universities in California now supportive of Antifa, which I can only half believe can be possible. But anyway we have had not only Antifa burning a police car in this country in Bristol, but also BLM toppling statues and painting Winston Churchill. People take to ideological thinking just as readily in the UK as in the USA. We are all equally readily infected with the same ideological pattern of thinking. Our BBC, the broadcasting company has adopted Wokery. Institutions, including universities and their students, are all welcoming to ideologies, students first, only just setting out their thinking, and, then the universities too! It is shameful, because it is intellectually corrupt. History is what it is. It can not be altered and it should not be attempted. Current behaviour is subject to criticism, but even that should not be subject to ideological thinking, which is to be avoided, and not because it recommends unwelcome conclusions but because ideological conclusions are inevitably all intellectually unsound, because of the ideological thinking.

CHAPTER 3 ALL OUR IDEOLOGIES

I don't know how many people alive today have ever opened Carl Marx's book "Das Kapital", now published with all the prefaces of all editions at five hundred and nineteen pages, in either the German editions of 1867,1873, 1883 or 1890, or the French edition of 1872, or even the English edition of 1886. I would think not very many or very much. If more had done so I think there would have been fewer Marxists. It is an intolerable mishmash. Marx's philosophical study of "Political Economy" is not about economics. He says so himself. It is about the philosophy of "Political Economy", the Politics of the Industrial Revolution in philosophical terms. He appears to have thought a philosophical treatment, like Hegel's philosophical treatment of Germany in the eighteenth century, would elevate the treatment of the economics of the industrial revolution in the nineteenth century to philosophical heights and outsmart the economists and financiers he despised and planned to denigrate. It therefore is philosophising about the political development of the factory system in the industrial revolution, principally in Britain and Germany. His analysis of matters usually regarded as economic are thus askew, and described in whimsical philosophical terms which make no sense at all. Economics are part of social history. The philosophical treatment of history is ideological par excellence. It simply isn't done any more today. It is, quite frankly, recognised nowadays as a methodical mistake. Of philosophy, which served mankind as intellectual pabulum for thousands of years, there is only logic left. Otherwise it is replaced by the latest science, Linguistics, which studies etymology, the historical development of the meanings in language and the phonology which has gone with it. Now that you can't give your history book any philosophical varnish, the subject has become less popular and has mostly died out. Anyway it is not a good living. Much of historical output is historical biography these days, and more biography than history.

In my day as an undergraduate, (after five years war service), in the 1940s, the study of history at university was still supposed to be tertiary education, and Hugh Trevor-Roper, the Regius Professor at Christ Church, Oxford was made Lord Dacre, even though he had made the error of recognising a forgery as Hitler's genuine diary. My tutor Alan (AJP)Taylor, at Magdalen College, Oxford, who had declared himself a Marxist while studying at Manchester (I think largely to tease his father who owned a cotton mill) and after post graduate studies in Czechoslovakia under the Communist Professor Pribram (who also taught Jan Masaryk, admired as a democrat who defied Hitler) Taylor wrote two books on European history, appalling

Marxist stuff all in dialectical terms, which he subsequently refused to allow to be published. I picked up second hand copies of both but they burnt with my house round them in 1969 and I can't even remember their titles now. It was while kitting out his two volumes with dialectical clothing that he referred to Das Kapital and discovered it was rubbish. Before, he had only read The Communist Manifesto, like most Marxists. I don't know if he condemned it as materialist philosophy and thus an inappropriate methodology for addressing economics, but I think he must have done. He could pick any theory to pieces, and later became a well known commentator on TV, lecturing for forty minutes without a note, or drawing breath, much as he had in schools in Oxford. There was a public interested in TV talks in those days. Not now. It is self expression on Facebook and Twitter these days, all of it unqualified expression of personal opinion. History and Greats (the Classics) were supposed to enable you to critique any body of knowledge or theorising, from your critical study of the various interpretations of your subject matter. You weren't adding facts to your basket, you were challenging them, and having your thinking challenged in turn by your tutor.

Nowadays universities have given up any pretence of this tertiary education and just continue secondary education, to give you the knowledge to pick up a job on leaving, or offering simple subjects without too much to learn for those coming up though quite unfit for further study, which the government is prepared to subsidise the universities to teach, to benefit industry, and taxes which is what provides funding for the politicians to direct to their projects. Now you exit your course just wrapped in an ideology, unaware of ideological thinking, your critical faculty undernourished and often withered away, your mind more of a spanner than a gauge.

This major change of culture across the West (USA and Britain anyway) has not been studied, it has happened without consideration. I was overseas, my career in diplomacy extinguished by Clement Attlee as Prime Minister when he became aware of the fraudulent Franco-German secret Nazi plot to establish Hitler's post war "Thousand Year European Fourth Reich" instead of the European Coal and Steel Community Treaty in 1950 but refused the Foreign Secretary Ernie Bevin's request to expose the plot in the British national press, on the grounds it would be too damaging for the UK Labour Party.

All the European countries in the EU can hardly have been unaware of the Nazism of the two Dictators and the Commission in Brussels, the French and German Presidents, who were known to be secretly Nazi in the British Foreign Office in 1950, whereas the French and German people were being re-educated in the occupation zones in democracy. They were sick of Nazism, it was just warfare and starvation for them. The commanders had enjoyed a charmed life and fed well. So they just carried on. The other elephant in the room in the next year, 1951, was the USA decided, in order to conduct the cold war, Germany must be re-established as a Nazi country again immediately, as a buffer against Soviet Communism. The USA ambassador hijacked the tripartite International Study Group on Germany (France, Britain and the USA, in the Foreign Office in London) convened to revise the occupation statutes for the three Allied Occupation Zones in Germany, of which I was Secretary General; and I found myself, to the astonishment of all concerned, for weeks taking the minutes as this plan was established, printing a hundred copies every night. Just as soon as we were done I handed in my resignation and in a week I was out. Many more officers in the FO planned to quit but no other actually did so, needing the job.

Burgess and MacLean left for Moscow a fortnight after I had walked out the front door and rung the Ministry of Defence from a telephone box in the street and volunteered to return to the army as a Korean volunteer, thinking it might anyway be best to die in a Nazi world. I have since decided it would be better to riposte, and the 60 Year National Secrecy is long past. I will guess President Joe Biden has heard of MacCarthyism but not of US Nazism in 1951.

He was eight years old. The USA did not know the French and German Presidents were simultaneously planning to topple the USA in due course, once they had got the United States of Europe, USE, together, as Attlee had concealed it. I don't think he looks that far ahead or back anyway. We diplomats did not think the United States of Europe would defeat the USA, we just thought it would punish us, and so far as the Nazi French and German Presidents are concerned that is about right so far; but the EU is now breaking up, the different economies in a single currency never a goer, only a Nazi would consider it. Nazis fancy that economics are subservient to the state. It comes from Marx's Das Kapital. The United States of Europe could fit in a single currency, but of course they are not fully united, just in the same club and reluctant to ever submit to German financial domination a second time, after their experience in world war 2; so France now just sees the EU as an opportunity to revenge Brexit and punish the UK for being on the winning side in the war.

Another philosophical treatment of history, like Marx's philosophical treatment of the nineteenth century was Oswald Spengler's 1921 "Downfall of the Western World", "Der Untergang den Abendlandes", a completely bogus ideology which identified civilisations, (Cultures), as having births, youths, vigour, learning, expansion and achievement, followed by obesity, old age, decadence, incapacity, followed eventually by final death and decay, just like life forms, cabbages and kings. Marx's "Das Capital" might similarly have been titled "The Debauch and Downfall of the Industrial Revolution and Western Civilisation". Spengler's book was Hitler's favourite philosophy reading. It was a classic example of ideological thinking, just made up to suit Spengler's mood. I have described him as the Butcher of Blankenberg. He taught school in Blankenberg-am-Rhein and published his ideology in 1921, disgruntled by the defeat of Germany in World War One, the defeat evidence of the decadent age of all Western civilisation, not just German Nazism. Ah well. He recommended in such an age we should all stop philosophising, now he had provided the final and conclusive one explaining it all, so no further thinking was required, and we should all just get on with engineering to improve living conditions, now the philosophy had been provided for us. Both books, Marx's and Spengler's, were brazen ideological concoctions. I was going to put in some quotes of Hegel's philosophising as well; but I don't think I will as nobody these days considers him unless they are, directly or indirectly, still Fascists.

It is not them I seek to influence but the modern Woke ideologists, who use the same ideological thinking that Hitler used, although quite unaware of it. They do still believe the Marxist ideology so I must first get stuck in to some of Marx's ideology from "Das Kapital", (the English 1885 version). Every bit is supposed to hang together, it is part of the pattern of any ideology, so it makes it difficult to pick a bit which does not rely upon another bit earlier in the book to make any sense. I want to find a text which stands on its own and can be seen to be an irrelevant philosophical concoction. Here is Chapter 3, starting at page 217, and I am taking just two pages from the over 500 of the book. His philosophical "Capital", the title of his book. could more appropriately be described as "The Philosophy of The Industrial Revolution". Any business needs Capital funding to get started and industry found itself suddenly in need of much more than was required for the prior manual cottage industry, small scale production at home. However for Marx, Capital included the machinery which enabled industry, and he used up a great deal of paper apportioning the capital "value" in the business between the goods (commodities), capital machinery, and wages (labour). The shares of value between these elements occupies chapter after chapter, floating between elements determined by the length of the working day and working week (which is nonsense; and marketing does not come into it either. He was a cottage industrialist making it all up without understanding, inventing "Surplus Value" instead). Marketing had not been named in those days, the cottage you had got your boots from was hardly a market, as an element influencing value, so value was simply inherent in the business and uninfluenced by any market element. That certainly provided more opportunity for philosophical analysis but made it infinitely less realistic. How was an element of value, surplus value, turned out to be picked by Marx as available for exploitation by the employer, largely dependent on the length of the working day and week, and how much this might be and who should enjoy it, and in what proportions? This has provided his grounds for social revolution. I was however quite unable to follow the manoeuvres he claimed for this surplus value, or to what exactly any such value was or could logically be surplus. It is a division of the value (the worth) of the business. Marx seems to be uncertain about it too, in so far as he gives it multiple analyses according to the length of the working week, in those days five and a half days or six or even seven full working days. It required a different calculation of the surplus value and it wasn't just a plus or minus calculation either. Why not?

Was he not really considering value as the funding available for all purposes, and if so it should surely have been addition and subtraction. I concluded he was in the grip of ideology and had unrealistic ideas which were terms in this ideology, a pattern of thinking which was as unrealistic as it was ideological. It may seem bold to dismiss him like this, but his dialectic is even more obviously ideological and simply wrong, an intellectual error, and is now long demolished as a simple confusion of the boundary line with the continuum, a distinction un-noticed until relatively recently when Bertrand Russell pointed it out. I have described it as the criterion/continuum, but I am inclined to join Bertrand Russell and discard the criterion, chiefly because I can't derive the original form of the word, so am not sure what it means.

Marx enjoyed churning out his ideological beliefs for forty years in the British Museum and took them to his grave, his mausoleum in Highgate. Without ideological conviction he could not have peddled such nonsensical fabrications with conviction. It will make Marxists cross to find his dialectic described as the boundary line/continuum muddle. But I think I know they can't actually make any sense of any of Das Kapital. Capital actually has a meaning, financial funding to launch an industrial business, or indeed any enterprise, and in German a number of subsidiary meanings, but with words added attached. To be blunt, it does not mean anything else. Marx used it as if it was the same as the Industrial Revolution and wrote a materialist philosophy about it. I think we should require a philosophy to be phrased in abstract terms, and administer stiff critiques of terms used. At best it is a misnomer of what lies between his covers. Cottage industries needed capital (for tools and materials) but industry needed hundreds or even thousands of times as much. Historically, mines always needed a lot initially, to dig the hole, but of course they could be dug slowly, theoretically by one man, but it was going to take him an excessively long time; and they lasted a long time and once dug the capital invested wasn't pre-eminent. Industry per contra was a rush, the production was valued so highly. A financial elite funded it. The banks weren't lending enough. Only the financial elite had sufficient credit; and only the British financial elite fully supported industry as soon as machinery was available. On the continent the elites kept their hands clean at first. That gave Great Britain a start, with a lead which lasted a hundred years. The British passed Factory Acts which ameliorated the severity of factory conditions. Marx pointed this out in Das Kapital, drawing attention to the fact if Germany did not do the same their future would be even worse for the working class than in Britain. In the United Kingdom Parliament was democratic, but in Germany the Kaiser was in command. That was why the German Parliament remained supine.

The fact Marxism is false doesn't mean employers in the nineteenth century were not unscrupulous and cruel as well as greedy. It only means Marx's thinking, his whole plan of attack, was awry. The Victorian age was a nightmare for any honest historian. We were quite uneducated for the changes thrust on society by the technological revolution which was introduced by machine industry and mass employment in close contiguity in the factories. My tutor, the late AJP Taylor, pointed out the only reason the health of the workers was not even worse than it was was because at least the factories were warm because of the contiguity of all the bodies in it. I told him as a child I had found in winter under the ivy on a wall in our garden literally hundreds of snails all stuck together in a single clump, a single mound of snailery more than a foot in diameter, and my father told me they were clinging together to share the warmth, so they didn't freeze.

Anyway when you get into the argument Marx's method is simply flawed, in so far as although he claims to be scientific he is nothing of the sort. It is a work of high philosophy but falls short of philosophic standards, because with materialist categories instead of abstract ones the free associations of philosophy are yet more absurd. The cost of production consists of the price of the commodities, and the value of the labour, what the workers are paid, which is treated as if it were a phenomenal item like the commodities. Well they are (whimsical) philosophic terms. The purpose of giving substance to the labour is so it can be divided up into value and surplus value. The employer snaffles the workers' surplus value, really due to the worker, that part of it attributable to his labour, calculable a dozen different ways according to the variable proportions of those elements ascribed to making up the whole value of the business. The more labour the more of the surplus value belonging to the worker which is not allocated to him by the employer. The employee is paid wages for the time that he is employed during the week, at a uniform rate. (Even Marx had not yet thought of overtime. His mind was in the cottage). But the bigger portion of the costs labour equals, the more of the surplus value shifts to the employee from the employer, who gets the bit for which the capital (machinery) and commodities (goods used up) are responsible. The entrepreneur contributes nothing, he is just a pestilence. You would never guess these initial entrepreneurs actually set up what is now known all across Europe as the industrial revolution, nor that it was destined to revolutionise the rate of improvement of, well just about everything, like when we learned to speak. These two leaps forward have never been rivalled. Marx rubbished industry and academia largely followed. These weren't academics you see. They were business makers who hadn't done much before, and you could argue they were inspired by the technologists who made the boilers and the machines. It all just came together without academia. Science made the machines, but it wasn't the theoretical scientists, it was entrepreneurial technical workers, learning how to measure power from the boilers. There isn't a mention of what these folk contributed in Marx's 550 pages, which were a philosophical rabbit cage. It would be unkind to suggest Marxist Socialists are still tending the same rabbit cage, but it is certainly a temptation.

In reality it was the coal, the steam power, and the power of the machinery to operate upon the material, of course, which was providing nine tenths of the total value, and Marx leaves them out. Early industry was labour intensive, but it was the intensity of everything else which resulted in the productivity of the output. A lever needed a hand to operate it but the hand was the easy bit. The set-up was the clever bit. Many of the workers' contributions were modest. Machinery went fast compared to a hand worker and there were a lot of machines, each one guided by a worker. Gradually time resulted in machines which combined the original machines increasing the production a single worker could guide. I think you should however argue more work was done by the machinery on its own rather than more by the worker's hand. Sorry! Then you might stop to realise both arguments were uncalled for. An entrepreneur should pay what can be paid and keep the company in trim. Now of course economic production is nothing like any of the initial industrialisation. Effectively machines run the machines and supervisors monitor the machines, and machines signal faults so monitors watch for signals that something has gone wrong. The more production the machinery produces the more can be paid for its supervision (and maintenance). Marx has nothing of this. I think it fair to say nothing Marx wrote was really relevant to industry when he wrote it and even less is it relevant today. It is not of much importance now if what he wrote was ever relevant, apart from the issue of his ideology and the skew it put on his thinking and his convictions, just as all ideological thinking does.

I am of course prejudiced, because I have demolished Marx's Dialectic, making use of Bertrand Russell's separation of the continuum from the boundary line, two straight lines Marx used as if they were the same. When you distinguish between the functions of these two lines the dialectic disappears, the Thesis, Antithesis and Synthesis which Marx, who planned to home in on his material philosophical approach and thus disprove the economists and financiers believed was a magic pattern (which I have instead described as an intellectual chain mail of coat-hanger-shaped thinking) which determined:-

(1). Human thinking,
(2). The way the world went.

So if you were thinking dialectically, your thinking matched the way the world went and so you would be right; whereas if you did not think dialectically you would be out of kilter with the way the world went, which could not help going the way it naturally did, and so you would be wrong.

Philosophy recognised philosophers and produced fresh flocks of ideologists prestigious in their day. Now they are properly viewed as merely playing cat's cradles with cascades of made-up philosophical terms. The following names are from Wikipedia:

(1) Forerunners Georg Hegel recognised: Aristotle, (Hegel prided himself on his Greek), and recent European philosophers Bohme, Spinosa, Rousseau, Kant, Goethe, Fichter, Holderlin, Schelling,

(2) Followers: Feuerbach, Marx, Stirner, Gentile, Lukaks, Kefever, Habermas.

This is of course a classic nest of ideological opinions. Every argument which self-guarantees correctness like this should today immediately fall under suspicion. You are in the embrace of ideology and are going to be right even when you are actually wrong. So it is necessary to dismiss this considerable chunk of culture en masse, more or less at a stroke. All our thinking for four hundred thousand years can be challenged similarly. We should perhaps interject this has nothing to do with Cancel Culture from Woke ideology, which far from wanting to dismiss our 400,000 years of ideological thinking is on the contrary based upon it entirely, and is more concerned in introducing Leftist thinking based on the Marxist dialectic and forgetting intellectual thinking, and just believing what you want. If you are Duchess Meghan you go one further and declare that as you believe, following the 1930s German philosopher Herbert Marcuse, there is no objective reality, you each have your own truth which you can make up. Since she is not a German historian, she must have got this absurd idea from the neo-Fascist ideology Antifa in California which had introduced Marcuse to free up their thinking. It is these ludicrous ideologies which the USA is currently serving up on the west which makes exposure of the universal ideological intellectual addiction urgently required, so humanity can regain its balance. The principal irrationality of Marcuse was, with no objectivity admitted, to presume nevertheless you were entitled to credibility just as if you were objective. You do indeed have to be pretty stupid to be able to believe that. If a view is not objective it is not objective. You can't have it subjective and objective, both at the same time. I think a three year old would agree you can't have a tadpole which is, at the same time, a fairy princess, don't you?

I have always enjoyed the story of Mr. Khrushchev in the United Nations. In an intense debate he took off his shoe and banged it on his desk - a historic insult in uncivilised societies. "We will destroy you all" he declared. He was thinking dialectically, so he was in sync with the world, and we weren't, so he was right and we weren't. With his shoe-banging he has ornamented my political thinking for decades. He leads the league of educated idiots – not that his education was anything much, but he was the leader of the Communist Soviet Union so his political experience you would have thought would have given him some know-how, especially how to avoid assassination. But no! all ideology gives you is illusion. When you face up to the issue you have to accept that since we first spoke, now acknowledged to have been at least four hundred thousand years ago, we have been following each other up, never right, always wrong, and improving our judgment (science) only slowly, totally unaware of our ideological thinking and its blockages of the light.

But meanwhile what on earth was Marx doing in the British Museum for forty years? The fact is he was setting up a revolutionary philosophy, or so he thought. What he was actually setting up was a champion ideology which would appeal to every other ideologist – and that was everyone else, although he did not know it, and nor did they – in order to give his ideology the prestige of Hegel's philosophical concoction; and indeed he could perhaps claim he succeeded in this. But he was introducing Hegelianism to a sphere, economics, which had immediate practical implications, and Socialism has been rowing in the wrong direction as a result for two hundred years and welcomes totalitarian thinking in aid of the class war when the true interest of the working class has always required a successful business economy. Unions planning to sabotage businesses any way they can have inevitably been sabotaging the working class. Marx's philosophised economics has involved an inevitable dialectical process which nevertheless has to be fought for, and has inevitably been won by those who have shunned the dialectic. It is a shame the workers have been so shabbily represented, by morons.

Take Sir Kier today. He is a lawyer! The High Court are all lawyers and remainers with the Nazi conspiracy which is the European Union to establish Hitler's post war "Thousand Year European Fourth Reich in order to establish the United States of Europe, USE, and eventually topple the USA so as to assume their political hegemony, although it is nearing both political and financial collapse.

The fact is Marx was really a down-to-earth man. The last thing he would fancy would be Georg Hegel's eighteenth century philosophic mind and idealist philosophical dialectic. Hegel himself had even gone so far as to suggest the dialectical process was a spiritual preconception of actual reality which would inevitably follow the spiritual pattern revealed by the dialectical categories. Three centuries ago thinking was a good deal wilder than would be considered today, even by ideologists. Hegel's spirit (geist) could also mean mind, mental. So his dialectical process could be regarded as a prior intellectual understanding of his philosophy, which determined the actuality in due course. All philosophy in fact, can now be seen to have been just a make-up of abstract categories, the acme of ideological thinking, and then making cat's cradles with them, with almost infinite rhetorical lecturing and publications following suit; in Hegel's case the majority written up from students' notes after his death. This philosophising was justified as reasoning to establish correct logic.

In Hegel's day logic comprised three divisions, doctrines of concept, judgment and inference. Doctrines of concept addressed the systematic hierarchical relations of the most general classes of things. Doctrines of judgment investigated relations of subject and predicate. And doctrines of inference laid out the forms of syllogisms originally found in the Aristotelian term logic. This tripartite hierarchical examination was philosophising in Hegel's day. Philosophy I suppose was for Hegel just intellectual methodology. Anyway he applied it to everything, with the ambition of relating his thinking to Kant's 1781 "Critique of Pure Reason", in which Kant had identified what he called the twelve pure ancestral concepts of the understanding that structure all experience irrespective of content. They were a priori. (You could not posit anything logically prior). The true ancestral concepts also had their equally pure derivative concepts! You can see he was entering an ant's nest of categories which could be shuffled together ad nauseum. It was another clear case of ideological thinking, abstract categories spilling out galore in personal mental patterns masquerading as a priori.

When you come to look at Hegel's philosophy, (or philosophies), there are problems. His thinking was prior to modern science, so he was fluent with ideas now not much followed except by modern philosophers of Fascism, blatantly or at one remove. In the eighteenth and nineteenth centuries the philosophical process was rule driven, a set of thinking schemes all actually completely ideological. It would probably be fair to say none of it had any real justification whatever. Even logic was an ideological composite with its three phases as already described above. Philosophy may have historically carried the human intellect forwards simply because it was the grounds for intellectual argumentation, but the categories philosophy generated, anyway for the most part, were unreal and lacked any justification. The new science of Linguistics has replaced it all with a modern scientific approach to the study of human language and human thinking. Linguistics impinges also on psychology and legalism, the law, and the ideological thinking they involve. For Linguistics all human thinking is ideological ever since we first spoke, not less than four hundred thousand years ago. It is not just the thinking pattern of historic ideologists like Hitler. We have all been guilty for the last four hundred thousand years, though Hitler was probably the nastiest thinker to date.

Hegel's adoption of the dialectic is nowadays challenged on the grounds his was not the crisp version with clearly identifiable terms, thesis, antithesis and synthesis that Marx thought it was, when he claimed to have stood Hegel on his head, with materialist elements engaged in the dialectical dance. Hegel himself attributed the dialectic to Kant. The current Marxist dialectic is the one to address because it is the one politically active. They are all equally wrong.

I was going to insert Hegel's books here (from Wikipedia), but what is the point? It was all philosophy, and now all out of favour with scientific linguistics.

But Marx himself said he had stood Hegel on his head and introduced a materialist dialectic with thesis, antithesis and synthesis in material terms, not just idealistic terms, and would thus use his philosophic arguments from Hegel to take economics upstairs and drag the economists out of their depth. He thought he had shed Hegel's spiritualism and rendered his materialist philosophy a down-to-earth methodology. But in reality it was no less an ideology than the Hegelianism he thought he had copied. His materialist terms had been taken upstairs where they became a philosophic miasma, far from real economics, on the contrary playing philosophic cat's cradles, the same as Hegel, but with material categories less suitable for such gaming.

All through his book he delights in out-manoeuvring and abusing the academic financiers and economists of the day; and he makes clear Das Kapital is not a system of economics but a "philosophy of political economy", with his quite frankly materialist philosophical terms which of course did not appear in the economic thought of the day, and equally, of course, not in economics today. Capital in economics was and is just the funding needed initially when setting up any business, which it is true had increased hundreds if not thousands of times, anyway astronomically, with the invention of the machinery which increased production astronomically too.

Das Kapital was for Marx the first term in his materialist philosophy which was going to supercede academic philosophy. He probably did not yet know it, but his materialist philosophy was just spinning the ideological hat out of which he could in due course pull his fabricated rabbits, (like surplus-value) for getting the dialectic to convict the employer of the day of wicked oppression of the worker in an inevitable natural process, which has provided socialists with their social theory ever since. But his philosophy has no more any reality than Hegel's. One imagines not many, perhaps not any, have ever struggled through Marx's 951 pages of Das Kapital, put together in forty years sitting in the British Museum, which gave him boils on his bottom. Capital became for him not just a sum of money but a philosophical term for what was more like the whole of the Industrial Revolution. Capitalism today has very little to do with the Industrial Revolution but is used to describe the economic system as it is today, a system with nothing to do with spinning machines or the extraction of metals from ores (his philosophical interchange of "Powers" between man and nature in this process occupying many pages). Metals are for Marx the synthesis of the ores and their antithesis the separation process (decomposition of the ore); and that is after the thetic earth and its antithetic (mined abstraction) of the synthetic ore, which then becomes the thetic term in the next dialectical process. Here is a neat example of how the world is built up as what I have described as a chain mail of coat-hangers, the arms of which, confronting each other, but connected together as the two-sided reality (earth and its dissolution), are synthesised in a process equivalent to the attachment of the hook in the middle (the ore) which then becomes the thetic term of the next dialectical process (extraction of the metal from the ore), the metal the synthesis of the ore and the extraction process). You should then not be surprised to find the metal ("in its pure form") as the thetic term in its manufacture (the human manufacture is the antithetic form of the thetic form of its initial purity). Human manufacture, with the impurity introduced by the industrial employer) is to render it a commodity with a use-value. This use-value is in turn a composite of all the use values of the previous dialectical processes, shared between the thetic term, with its capital value, and the antithetical term, the processing or labour-value). So now you can see the coat-hanger chain mail thinking is the vehicle for the mixes of values.

To match Das Kapital in its absurdity as the industrial process was his description of value in terms which enabled him to produce (like a rabbit out of his value-hat) a "Surplus-Value" inhabiting any business – so what on earth is it? – it is a philosophical term which can be manipulated according to the other elements of Marx's philosophic political economy (not all that many). Das Kapital was political philosophy and not economics at all, as indeed Marx himself was to point out within his book. He thought a philosophical backing was a virtue, and it had taken him a good deal of effort to set the whole revolutionary materialist philosophy up. You could say that was what he had been up to for the forty years, drafting and redrafting to make sure it all matched up – he described the redrafting as "stylistic". Nobody had thought of the trick before, making up a philosophy to carry a political economy. They had used whatever was around already. Marx opened up the pull of ideological thinking for generations. His philosophy still underlies most if not all ideological thinking from both Hitler and Stalin

(Hitler was a Marxist, a National Socialist, not an extreme right thinker, that is a fabrication by post-war Europe to give Socialism, with much of the ideological thinking of Nazism, a bit of clear water between Socialism and the Holocaust (which it hardly deserves). There was nothing Conservative about Nazism. Admittedly Hitler was anti-Communist. If Russia had not been Communist Hitler could have been Communist as well as Nazi. It's that simple. The US Democratic Party is Socialist (Marxist}, even today, and all these latest ideologies, Antifa, BLM, Cancel Culture, emanating from California, are Marxist too. I will bet nobody alive today (in California or elsewhere) has read Das Kapital or the English or French translations, certainly not fully. Like Mr. Khrushchev they are shoe bangers. They don't read much, or don't think much if they do.

Prime Minister Attlee in Great Britain in 1950, refused to publish the news, as Foreign Secretary Ernie Bevin urged him to do, of the Nazi plot in the terms of the negotiation of the European Coal and Steel Community Treaty betrayed to us, because it would show too close a relationship between Nazism and Socialism, when the secret codicils in the Franco-German European Coal and Steel Community Treaty, nominally set up to stop economic warfare, which instead secretly provided for Hitler's post war Thousand Year European Fourth Reich – the French and German Presidents, but not the people, were still Nazi, as known to MI6 (Pat Reilley), the government of the day, and me, as I was already in the British Foreign Office, in 1950, in the German Political Department, after 5 years war service, Nobody else in the Foreign Office in 1950 is left alive today and I am fortunate to still have all my marbles. I should mention also in 1951 the USA ordered the Allies (the USA were the only ones to come out of the war with any money) to reinstate NAZI Germany immediately as a bulwark against Russian Communism in the Cold War. I dare say President Joe Biden knows about McCarthyism in the USA in 1950, but I will bet he knows nothing of this Nazism in the USA in 1951. He was eight years old.

Europe was simultaneously concealing an absurd Nazi conspiracy in due course to topple the USA. It still is, but in reality is about to break apart as it becomes apparent the democracy in the EU is fraudulent and the French and German presidents are the joint Dictators of Europe running the Commission in Brussels and lying firmly every day, as Dr. Goebbels recommended, and have been for over seventy years. Europeans in 16 countries have now recently issued a Joint Declaration the EU is too totalitarian and is overdue for radical reform, and sent it to Brussels. I agree. I resigned in 1951. Better late than never for Europe. No Democracy has a Commission. The EU Constitution was written by Dr. Goebbels in 1943 for Hitler's post war Thousand Year European

Fourth Reich. It was copied by the German war criminals imprisoned by the international court at Nuremberg from the Nazi archive in Berlin when the USA let them all out again in 1951, to reinstate Nazi Germany; and they posted it to Brussels where the Commission adopted it all, at once, and without consulting Europe. MEPs have no power to pass any laws of their own, only to approve regulations sent down to them by the Commission (told they approve them!).

Now here is page 216 of Das Kapital which I think gives you a fair idea of the gist of his ridiculous ideological magnum opus, converting economics into a philosophy based on Hegel's. It makes no sense.

"PART 3. THE PRODUCTION OF ABSOLUTE SURPLUS VALUE.

CHAPTER 7. THE LABOUR PROCESS AND THE PROCESS OF PRODUCING SURPLUS VALUE.

Section 1: The Labour Process or the Production of Use Value.

[You can see he knew he was writing new (philosophical) stuff he had made up, from the elaborate introductory headings].

"The capitalist buys labour-power in order to use it, and labour-power in use is Labour itself. [cp. Kant's thing-in-itself or for-itself, Hegel also believed the same. [This opening sentence already indicates the absurdity of the ideological thinking]. The purchaser of labour-power consumes it by setting the labourer to work. [This purchase of labour-power is actually of course just the wages paid to the worker, the simple transaction transposed to a purchase and consumption of a prior power, or geist, to fit in with the terms of the dialectical ideology. It is a confusion, not a valid analysis]. By working, the labourer becomes actually what before he only was potentially, labour-power in action, a labourer. [What do we learn by describing work as labour-power in action? Nothing!] In order that his labour may reappear in a commodity he must before all things expend it on something useful, on something capable of satisfying a want of some sort. Hence what the capitalist sets the labourer to produce, is a particular use-value, a specified article. The fact that the production of use-values, or goods, is carried on under the control of a capitalist and on his behalf, does not alter the general character of that production. We shall therefore, in the first place, have to consider the labour process independently of the particular form it assumes under given social conditions. [Sciat: nothing is contributed in the labour process by the capitalist, there is just the manual labour of the worker responsible for the product, which we are going to consider].

Labour is, in the first place, a process in which both man and nature participate, and in which man of his own accord, starts, regulates and controls the material reactions between himself and Nature. He opposes himself to Nature as one of her own forces, setting in motion arms and legs, heads and hands, the natural forces of his body, in order to appropriate Nature's productions in a form adapted to his own wants. By thus acting on the external world and changing it, he at the same time changes his own nature. He develops his slumbering Powers and compels them to act in obedience to his Sway. We are not now dealing with those primitive instinctive forms of labour that remind us of the mere animal. An immeasurable interval of time separates the state of things in which a man brings his labour-power to market for sale as a commodity, from that state in which human labour was still in its first instinctive stage. We presuppose labour in a form that stamps it as exclusively human. A spider conducts operations which resemble those of a weaver, and a bee puts to shame many an architect in the construction of its cells. But what distinguishes the worst architect from the best of bees is this, that the architect raises his structure in imagination [geist!] before he erects it in reality. At the end of every labour process we get a result which already existed in the imagination of the labourer at its commencement. He not only effects a change of form in the material on which he works but he realises a purpose of his own that gives the law to his modus operandi, and to which he must subordinate his will. And this subordination is no mere momentary act. Besides the exertion of the bodily organs, the process demands that, during the whole operation, the workman's will be steadily in consonance with his purpose. This means close attention. The less he is attracted by the nature of the work, and the mode in which it is carried on, and the less therefore he enjoys it as something which gives play to his bodily and mental powers, the more close his attention is forced to be. [These are all otiose spiritual/mental (dialectical) transactions, immaterial, with no reality. It was the nature of philosophy at that time. None of it is current except in Marxism, and only there because all Marxists are inveterate ideologists, incapable of seeing outside their ideological thinking].

The elementary factors of the labour process are 1, the personal activity of man, i.e., work itself, 2, the subject of that work, and 3, its instruments.

The soil (and this economically speaking includes water) in the virgin state in which it supplies man with necessaries or the means of subsistence ready to hand, exists independently of him and is the universal subject of human labour. All those things which labour merely separates from immediate connexion with their environment are subjects of labour spontaneously provided by Nature. Such are fish which we catch and take from their element, water, timber which we fell in the virgin forest, and ores which we extract from their veins. [Do ores have veins?]. If on the other hand the subject of labour has, so to say, been filtered through previous labour, we call it raw material, such is ore already extracted and ready for washing. All raw material is the subject of labour, but not every subject of labour is raw material. It can only become so after it has undergone some alteration, by means of labour.

An instrument of labour is a thing, or a complex of things, which the labourer interposes between himself and the subject of his labour, and which serves as the conductor of his activity. He makes use of the mechanical, physical, and chemical properties of some substances in order to make use of other substances subservient to his aims. Leaving out of consideration such ready-made means of subsistence as fruits, in gathering which a man's own limbs serve as the instruments of his labour, the first thing of which a labourer possesses himself is not the subject of labour but it's instrument. Thus Nature becomes one of the organs of his activity, one that he annexes to his own bodily organs, adding stature to himself in spite of the Bible. [What on earth is this reference to the Bible?] As the earth is his original larder, so too is it his original tool house. It supplies him for instance with stones, for throwing, grinding, pressing, cutting, etc. The earth itself is an instrument of labour, but when used as such in agriculture implies a whole series of other instruments and a comparatively high development of labour. No sooner does labour undergo the least development, than it requires specially prepared instruments. Thus in the oldest caves we find stone implements and weapons. In the earliest period of human history, domesticated animals, i.e. animals which have been bred for the purpose, and have undergone modifications by means of labour, play the chief part as instruments of labour along with specially prepared stones, wood, bones, and shells. The use and fabrication of instruments of labour, although existing in the germ among certain species of animals is specifically characteristic of the human labour-process, and Franklin therefore defines man as a tool-making animal. Relics of bygone instruments of labour possess the same importance for investigation of extinct economic forms of society".

There is another three pages of this but it is a repetitious theorising in terms of use-values, which are in reality the total costs of production of the commodities produced. The use-value actually "is" the commodity, or anyway its doppelganger, the mental thing-in-itself, or as I believe Kant originally thought of it as the thing-for-itself, the pure stuff without any empirical monkeying. So I am going to skip three pages. Then we come to the subheading "Section 2. The Production of Surplus-Value", which reveals to me is just the way he defines the profit on sale of the commodity, as if it were an actual entity manufactured by the labour=process alongside the commodity produced, which must now be installed alongside the use-value, the production costs It means, of course, the profit is manufactured by the worker as he manufactures the goods, nothing to do with the market. In reality the profit the capitalist makes is determined by the market. Goods may sell for more or less than they cost to produce, and this is of course is the essence of modern capitalism, with competition between entrepreneurs providing the check on increase of prices which has conditioned the actual progress and prosperity of all classes. There is no recognition of any of this in Das Capital, only the sham materialist philosophical categories to provide a dialectical process which can be used to make up an ideological set of terms which can carry whatever conclusions the ideologist seeks. It certainly appears as if Marx was quite unaware of the essential nature of economic capitalism based on mechanical industry, on which he spent forty years concocting a fraudulent scheme of ideological thinking, what he called a "materialist philosophy" based on what he believed was Georg Hegel's dialectic, which he claimed he had "stood on its head" with his materialist categories in place of Hegel's idealist ones. Now it is generally recognised Hegel's philosophy was not the full dialectical process Kant had conceived in the previous century and recorded in his "History of Pure Reason" and the pattern which Marx actually copied, (stood on its head).

Anyway here is Section 2 on page 130: "The product appropriated by the capitalist is a use-value, as yarn, for example, or boots. But, although boots are, in one sense, the basis of all social progress, and our capitalist is a decided "progressist", yet he does not manufacture boots for their own sake. Use-value is by no means the thing "qu'on aime pour lui meme" [French: "which one likes for itself"] in the production of commodities. Use-values are only produced by capitalists because, and in so far as they are the material substratum, depositories of exchange-value. [The cobbler in the cottage industry preceding machine industry sold his footwear too, no difference here. Admittedly he wore it too, but for many years he sold it all]. Our capitalist has two objects in view, in the first place to produce a use-value which has a value in exchange, that is to say an article destined to be sold, a commodity, and secondly he desires to produce a commodity whose value shall be greater than the values of the commodities used in its production, that is of the means of production of the labour-power that he purchased with his good money in the open market. His aim is to produce not only a use-value but a commodity also, not only use-value but value, not only value, but at the same time surplus-value".

With the introduction of all these serial values the grammar seems to slip a bit in the last two sentences. We have use-value, and exchange value (on sale), and in the second sentence the exchange value has become a commodity (goods for sale), introducing an exchange-value once

130

again. Should it not really read "not only use-value but exchange-value, not only (the exchange) value, but surplus-value". He is trying to smuggle in this surplus-value in addition to the exchange value, both of them surplus to the (honest) use-value, the cost of production. Both the exchange value and the surplus-value are really determined by the market which is not part of the production process or cost of production, and as far as I can see are really the same value, the exchange value being the sum of the use-value and the additional value in the market, and the surplus-value being just the additional value of the market value. He has two values, the exchange value and the surplus-value, in order to describe the market value as part of the production process. He is apparently using an intermediary unspecified "value", so as to raise the additional surplus value as if it were not already included in the exchange-value. This is important, as it is the surplus-value he has actually extracted out of the exchange-value that plays a large part in the remaining 415 pages, which suggest the capitalist (sc. entrepreneur) has stolen it from the labourer. Well. it has been hopped forward from labour-value via exchange-value to surplus-value, with the two critical sentences above, which as actually published appear to be gibberish and can only make sense if value is corrected to exchange-value, when surplus-value is thereupon revealed as the same as the profit which has been lurking all the time in exchange-value, which Marx has derived in turn from labour-value. The neutral unspecified "value" is apparently interposed to achieve this duplication. It is also of general interest in so far as all ideological thinking allows this kind of adjustment of terms to confirm a desired belief. It is classic ideology. Everything in Hegel's idealist philosophy was just ideology, his own fabrication, empty chat; and Marx's improvement was no better. In fact it was worse.

Do we want any more of section 2, of this materialist philosophy of political economy, which Marx thought was appropriately titled Capital, Das Kapital? We have discovered the origin of Surplus-Value. I don't think we really do. However It goes on as follows to show its absurdity:

"It must be borne in mind, that we are now dealing with the production of commodities and that, up to this point, we have only considered one aspect of this process. Just as commodities are, at the same time, use-values and values, so the process of producing them must be a labour-process, and at the same time a process of creating value. [Not a bit of it. The extra value of exchange-value is actually determined by the market. It can be a minus quantity, but both cottage industry and mechanical industry took care to avoid this]. Let us now examine production as a creation of value.

We know that the value of each commodity is determined by the quantity of labour expended on and materialised in it, by the working time necessary under given social conditions, for its production. This rule also holds good in the case of the product that accrued to our capitalist as a result of the labour process carried on for him. Assuming this product is to be 10 lbs of yarn, our first step is to calculate the quantity of labour realised in it.

For spinning the yarn, raw material is required, suppose in this case 10 lbs of cotton. We have no need at present to investigate the value of this cotton, for the capitalist has, we will assume, bought it at its full value, say of ten shillings. In this price the labour required for the production of the cotton is already expressed in terms of the average labour of society. We will further assume that the wear and tear of the spindle, which, for our present purpose, may represent all other instruments of labour employed, amounts to the value of 2s. [two shillings]. If, then, 24 hours' labour, or two working days, are required to produce the quantity of gold represented by twelve shillings, we have here, to begin with, two days' labour already incorporated in the yarn.

We must not let ourselves be misled by the circumstance that the cotton has taken a new shape while the substance of the spindle has to a certain extent been used up. By the general law of value, if the value of 40 lbs of yarn - the value of 40 lbs of cotton – the value of a whole spindle, i.e. if the same working time is required to produce the commodities on either side of this equation, then 10 lbs of yarn are an equivalent of 10 lbs of cotton, together with one fourth of a spindle. In the case we are considering the same working-time is materialised in the 10 lbs of yarn on the one hand and in the 10 lbs of cotton and the fraction of a spindle on the other. Therefore, whether value appears in cotton, in a spindle, or in yarn, makes no difference to the amount of that value. The spindle and cotton, instead of resting quietly side by side, join together in the process, their forms are altered and they are turned into yarn, but their value is no more affected by this fact than it would be if they had been simply exchanged for their equivalent in yarn.

The labour required for the production of the cotton, the raw material of the yarn, is part of the labour necessary to produce the yarn, and is therefore contained in the yarn. The same applies to the labour embodied in the spindle without whose wear and tear the cotton could not be spun.

Hence, in determining the value of the yarn, or the labour-time required for its production, all the special processes carried on at various times and at different places which were necessary, first to produce the cotton and the wasted portion of the spindle, and then with the cotton and spindle, and then with the cotton and spindle to spin the yarn, may together be looked on as different and successive phases of one and the same process. The whole of the labour in the yarn is past labour, and it is a matter of no importance that the operations necessary for the production of its constituent elements were carried on at times which, referred to the present, are more remote than the final operation of spinning. If a definite quantity of labour, say thirty days, is required to build a house, the total amount of labour incorporated in it is not affected by the fact that the work of the last day is done twenty nine days later than that of the first. [These were evidently workers' houses, just wooden sheds, completed in thirty days. My cow sheds took longer than this, they had brick walls for warmth, mangers and hay racks, concrete floors and drains, with double doors, and the roofs were tiled the same as houses, and cows needed milking parlours as well]. Therefore the labour contained in the raw material and the instruments of labour can be treated just as if it were labour expended in an earlier stage of the spinning process, before the labour of actual spinning commenced.

The value of the means of production, i.e. the cotton and the spindle, which values are expressed in the price of twelve shillings, are therefore constituent parts of the value of the yarn, or in other words of the product.

Two conditions must nevertheless be fulfilled. First the cotton and spindle must concur in the production of a use-value, they must in the present case become yarn. Value is independent of the particular use-value by which it is borne, but it must be embodied in a use-value of some kind. Secondly, the time occupied in the labour of production must not exceed the time really necessary under the given social conditions of the case. Therefore, if no more than 1 lb of cotton be required to spin 1 lb of yarn, care must be taken that no more than this weight of cotton is consumed in the production of 1 lb of yarn, and similarly with regard to the spindle. Though the capitalist have a hobby and use a gold instead of a Steel spindle, yet the only labour that counts for anything in the value of the yarn is that which would be required to produce a Steel spindle, because no more is necessary under the given social conditions". [There's a clever bit of thinking. But how many gold spindles were there?]

There are another seven pages of this, but I will not give more of it room. We have introduced "the Process of Producing Surplus-Value", which was the purpose of the chapter, already, in the first three pages, and all the remainder appear to me to be merely philosophical fillers, so I am inclined to leave them out after showing some off. I believe the gist of the whole work, which Marx spent forty years on, was to produce a volume of (materialist) philosophical reasoning sufficient to deter any critics from examining the whole of it in detail, and indeed putting it out of the intellectual reach of the economists of the day, who will not have cared to take on a voluminous study of political economy, based upon the philosophy of Professor Hegel - quite frankly, who would? To me the whole project of Das Kapital seems to be bunkum, which was coined in the United States from a Mr Walker, representative for the constituency of Buncombe, who spoke for hours, without a break, in order to have the motion he opposed run out of time, finishing up by making up sentences, simply to keep going. He just needed the volume, not the meaning. There is a lot of bunkum in all of us, better described as ideology, blathering on and on, adding nothing, but just more and more of the same stuff we have actually made up from what we think we know. Mr Walker claimed he was speaking for Buncombe, and he was taken at his word. Bunkum was added to the English dictionary. It was just in time for Karl Marx; but only now used.

The next chapter of Das Kapital, Chapter 8, is headed "Constant Capital and Variable Capital". But we can not go on copying the 500 pages put there, as I say, apparently as a block on discussion. There is certainly no wisdom in any of this, only a revamp of Hegel's philosophy, now disregarded, except as a historical curiosity, with even less warrant dressed in materialist terms than as recited in intellectual terms by

Hegel. Marx's materialist re-arrangement really required a material geist for his material dialectic and material geists are hard to come by.

I have done my best to get my mind round Das Kapital. I think it leaves it damaged beyond repair. As I say, it looks to me as if Marx's aim was to build a mountain nobody would be prepared to climb. If he believed he was adding wisdom to ordinary economics, it merely makes him that much more ill-informed. There is nothing surprising in that. Hundreds of years ago, everyone was ill-informed. Everyone thought philosophising was the best way to go about thinking anything out. We all thought ideologically as a matter of course, and at the same time were quite unaware of it. We always had done, ever since we first learned to speak. Those with the most ideas were the most ill-informed. I am not doing any more on Marx.

The interesting thing is everyone thinking ideologically with their own mini ideologies today, like those emanating from California, all seem to derive support from Marx. They are Marxists too. They tend to pick up the common ideological pattern from him. They don't have to do any thinking of their own at all for that. They just slip into the Marxist pattern and away they go, on woke stuff urging violence – not quite international revolution in order to destroy all social classes except the only honest class, the working class, with no property to defend; but destructive of property, burning it, making a mockery of history and denying any merit in culture, all uncivilised postures nobody not trapped in their ideological misunderstanding of human thinking would consider for a moment. They do make it hard to follow any Socialist policies any more, especially since their Marxist dialectic has been demolished, just an ideological confusion of the boundary line with the continuum. When they are separated the dialectic, with its thesis, antithesis, synthesis simply disappears. Nearly three hundred years of political thinking is rubbished at a stroke. Dialectical thinking is wrong. The dialectic pattern (Thesis, antithesis, synthesis) has never happened and never happens. It is an ideological error.

I am of course indebted to Professor Richard Overy's eight hundred and forty-eight page work, "The Dictators" published in 2004, which examines at length the ideologies of Hitler and Stalin, with much the same, and much different. In both regimes people were herded into camps, labour camps as well as extermination camps (Concentration Camps and the Gu-Lag) and prison camps and prisoner of war camps, hundreds and hundreds of them, in both Germany and Russia. By the end of the war in Europe the male population, and a substantial proportion of the female population was by then in displaced person camps and it took five years for the Allies to get the population fed and out of their DP camps and back into their own countries. As a brand new diplomat I was employed conducting retirees from the Lords on what you could really only regard as jollies visiting the Kreis in the British Zone to see the democracy being installed and for the Kreis to show it off. A good deal of German wine was shown off too. This was while presidential fraudulence was being revealed to MI6 of course. I was introduced to the geography at the same time as the German liquor.

Professor Overy quotes Hans Kohn in 1949, and I think I must do the same:

"In Russia and Germany – and wherever totalitarianism penetrated – men were fired by a fanatical faith, by the absolute unquestioning certainties which rejected the critical attitudes of modern man. Total fanaticism in Russia and Germany broke the dykes of civilisation which the nineteenth century had believed lasting".

This totalitarianism of course is one of the markers which identifies ideological thinking. But Kohn does not recognise this ideological thinking as such. Professor Overy does. But he is still far from recognising ideological thinking as the universal elephant in the room which it is. This was of course because the criminal totalitarian ideologies of the Nazis and Communists were outstandingly abhorrent, making them effectively criminally insane, along with all their leaders, and followers. But then there are no obvious boundaries of sanity. In so far as ideological thinking has been the habit of all mankind, ever since we first spoke, some four hundred thousand years ago, and we have all been unaware of it all along, you could argue we have all been effectively insane all along. Our scientific as well as our religious thinking has all been in ideological terms. How many sciences have there been since we spoke, and have not scientists and religionists killed those wanting to introduce new ideas not entirely consonant with the current ideology. When Professor Vellikovsky of the university of Tel Aviv who had new ideas about the orbit of Venus which he believed was originally a comet, captured by the sun, which as it gradually established its planetary orbit was responsible for the last Ice Age and its melting told Einstein that he had been persecuted by the principal American astronomer of the day, so his books had had to be published in England, Einstein just said "I know". He did not mean he knew about the books, but about the malice of those defending their ideological belief in their thinking.

Before we spoke we could have thought only in terms of pictures and emotions, of which we would have had no index to help our sentiments, as we had no words to express and record our thinking in order to recall it. In these circumstances we certainly do have to start thinking about our thinking. Speaking today is not just a bit, and certainly not a lot more of the same. We are in a different world altogether, which we have gradually (exceedingly gradually) built up, over four hundred thousand years, as a human verbal whimsey, which has actually composed our world image, all of it, and the science extracted from it, which has taken us to the moon and back.

Scientific Linguistics introduces us to a complete rehash of our thinking. Before we spoke, thinking was much more difficult. In fact it was too difficult for us to get much of it done. Once we got speaking started, the pace at which language built up reminds me of the formation of flints in a bed of sand or stalactites in a cave, although it had the actual physical characteristics of neither of these. It was an intellectual performance, not a process at all, more a whimsical happenstance than anything, as we developed the intellectuality of our minds. Our intellectuality dripped into our minds as the flint dripped into the sand, or down the stalactite in the cave. This modern scientific linguistics is a complete rehash of our philosophical linguistics as practised at MIT, where Professor Noam Chomsky has diverted the science to the world wide philosophical study of his transformational grammar for fifty years, but scientific linguistics is the denigration of philosophies of all sorts and kinds as ideological perversions of rationality.

I want now to look at some other ideologies, in religion and politics, and in events, unwinding on a daily basis because of ideological thinking - such as one reads every day in the newspapers.

Ideologies tend to have guard dogs (human ones). You can not expect to identify their thinking as ideological, and therefore quite misleading, without getting a hostile press.

My only defence is of course by showing by way of their common characters, that their thinking is all related, and they have a common ideological thinking which becomes apparent, which in turn renders their thinking wrong. Almost unbelievably, this ideological thinking dates from when we were learning to speak, and that is now generally accepted as at least four hundred thousand years ago. Our need to devise a scheme to get everyone thinking of the same meanings for the sounds, as we learned to utter them, had to be solved. How?

This was the major problem when setting language up. A language which did not have the same meanings for all its speakers was a very poor language, in fact it was no language at all, it was completely useless. As we had no language at the time we could not discuss the matter. We had a developed way of intercommunicating, of course, but it was limited: gestures, pointing – I suppose we would now say body language. What about shaking the head? Was yes up and down and no from side to side before speech? Did we shake our fists, and wave people to come or go away? I will guess men knew how to indicate their desires. Did you wave a spear to get a party of men to go hunting with you?

Body language inevitably had a limited coverage. These first meanings obviously did not include developed thinking. That came later, possibly thousands of years later, we shall never know; and the first agreed terms were merely individual meanings for the individual phonemes, as we learned to utter and identify them, (what are now just the twenty-six single letters of the alphabet), stripped of their meanings now we have words, endlessly more complex, originally made up from strings of constituent meaningful phonemes.

I have reviewed these twenty-six phonemes and the individual meanings we gave them four hundred thousand years ago, in my books on Linguistics. I have shown that in order to provide a theme to get everyone giving the same meanings to the phonemes, we adopted what was strictly an ideological prevarication. We made out phonemes had the meaning of the same sound made in nature: or in other words, using terms not available at the time, the meaning of each phoneme was echoic. This was, in fact, where language adopted what is now ideology, because the sounds in nature adopted were not really echoic of the phonemes, or the phonemes echoic of the sounds in nature we decided they were, so this approximation was introduced as crucial to our thinking, and it still is, and this ideology now allows far too much composition of a virtual reality which is imaginary, just as we found ourselves doing when we first spoke. That was when we had to search for some kind of principle which would inform each one of us of common meanings. We had no vocabulary of ideas to help us, which of course enables us to come along four hundred thousand years later and repeat their search in much the same ill-informed way. Just don't allow any ideas from four hundred thousand years of language to intrude – well, just try and manage without any ideas to guide you. What prompt is immanent in each phoneme? We would say today, it's phonology, how its sound struck us. After twenty years debating the matter with myself and still feeling somewhat uncertain I was right, I decided the reason it was so hard to guess the solution we adopted was because there actually was only one single way possible, and since this was so, that must have been the way we had adopted, else we would still be dumb. So if you can think of another way, do please let me know. Everyone else, of course, academia all together, have all declared it an impossible job; and after some ideological phantasmagorias invented without much merit from bibliophiles in the nineteenth century, it was declared impossible and it should therefore never be attempted again. So far as I know that has reduced competition entirely, and it was not until I had retired from three consecutive careers at seventy-three years of age that I began to ponder what, if anything, might be possible.

I had the unusual advantage of having spent two years in the Malayan jungle hunting terrorists, between 1954 and 1956, working closely with the Senoi aboriginal tribes and studying their language, which amounted to only three hundred words, at that time only known to a few civil servants in the department of the Malayan government appointed to ensure their survival; and as you can imagine their words were of quite general meanings; and conversation was laboured because of the polysemy the words carried, as well as the quite different way from Malay they put their words together. And, I said to myself at the time, they have gradually added all that, so they certainly had a great deal less when they first started - I had no idea how long ago at the time, and never thought of thinking about it. So far as their civilised Malay neighbours, outside the jungle, were concerned, they ignored the Senoi, not much caring to have aboriginal cousins, and had never learned their language. In reality the Senoi were not cousins. They had walked thousands of miles to find empty lebensraum thousands of years ago. The head man at one long house was good enough to invite me to join his tribe and he would give me their two shoulder tattoos and drill my nose to take a porcupine quill. I had my shirt off for the tattoo when we were called away following up a contact in the jungle with terrorists. I still have the porcupine quill, but no hole in my nose. Aboriginal boys have a pin hole and put expanding grass stalks in to enlarge it as they grow up.

It doesn't matter too much how right I am about our original individual meanings. What is important is the habit we evidently picked up of inventing a whole ideological phantasmagoria of ideas on very little evidence, and none of it in the least scientific, and then holding all of the intellectual scheme resulting to be essential, and effectively sacred, because if adulterated all understanding would fall to pieces. This ideology will have been the case when we were putting our language together based on a supposed echoism, which barely obtained in any really meaningful sense, but it established a pattern of ideological thinking, starting out with a basic presumption which (we felt) confronted a predicament which we had identified as a serious threat to our survival and wellbeing, a traumatic stress which had captured our minds - the original traumatic stress was how to get our meanings agreed. When you consider we had been speechless for ever, I suppose you could just call the feeling PTSD (Post Traumatic Stress Disorder). These days suicide is just another ideology, much like any other. Ideologies are classical thinking, but invalid. This is what humanity has to get under its belt. I have described it as the elephant in the room, because it is an ideational scheme to which every one of us with language is wedded. We are all potential ideologists, not just Hitler and other totalitarian dictators. Ideological thinking is not just a mistaken philosophy, it is a whole methodology of thinking which is misleading and needs to be identified and replaced worldwide. Once you get the idea it isn't hard. Just don't let your mind adopt the ideological non-sequiturs; make sure the first one does actually sequit (follow) [from the reality] before adopting it.

In this collection of ideologies we should also include the Communist ideology and the Chinese totalitarian tyranny with capitalist associations, but they teach us little beyond Marx. Their totalitarian ideology (self-deception) is just as absurd as his, in spite of the improvement in scientific thinking since. That won't stop them imposing their ideologies, which is why ideology must be put in its place. There are plenty of other ideologies which stand out, as well as more which are in use but are not all that important. My son when very young had an ideological belief his marbles had been stolen. They were found in a different pocket some days later. His ideological belief had essential ingredients: a traumatic grievance, a firm belief in the factual accuracy of the belief, a refusal to consider anything outside the ideology (although it proved to apply, namely they were in that other pocket), a determination to pursue the matter, a readiness to exert extreme measures in order to achieve the outcome desired. Several other small boys at the local school were probably in some danger. Well, you can see how Hitler behaved too. I will define ideological thinking as precisely as I can in Chapter 5 and the book must then be published so everyone can see how their thinking is betrayed at the drop of a hat, and hopefully will learn to mend their ways. Ideologists will all be confronted, every one of us at once.

I already mentioned Napoleon Buonaparte, and I have suggested his ideology was triggered by the bloodshed of the French revolution. The guillotine was justified by the beliefs of the revolutionaries, engaged in ideological thinking. We can not review French history here, but the violence of the thinking of so many was astonishing. They were all locked into their ideologies which rendered them impervious to thinking outside the loop, which included Madame Guillotine. I have already covered quite a bit of philosophy in this chapter. All of it is ideological. Philosophers are wed to ideological thinking. It is their intellectual livelihood. They generate their own trauma. Just the ordinary pressures of living are sufficient to set them off. Socrates insisted on masturbating in public in the market place and was sentenced to death for corrupting the youth of the nation. He conceded nothing, what he was doing was right. What was it? I am just guessing, but I think he thought it was essential to be completely open, that is to say not to have any inhibitions. The Woke ideologies are the same. What will we find next in California? Or with Stonewall? We are all supposed to admire Socrates because of his bravery in the face of death. Aristotle believed women were mortal and only men could look forward to an afterlife. It was a degree of misogyny virtually unmatched in the human record, although female circumcision must come near. The legal profession copy his thinking today. We should be thankful they do not also copy his thinking about women. Well, we must hope they all don't. The law is all ideological thinking. The Supreme Court admires the Nazi European Union because with our parliament subject to European law they got the over-riding European law sent to them by the European international court, regardless of parliament, and parliament was subject to it! They were thus able to impose their will on parliament, so long as it was a Will formed in the EU. Their ideology is a Nazi ideology. We would do far better with the supreme court returned to the House of Lords, where the lords are certainly no brighter but do have more understanding of their own limitations. That way we would risk having a Socialist supreme court in place of a National Socialist one. There is not as much difference between the two as socialists like to pretend. The Socialist State outranks the citizen, there is an element of totalitarianism in it. Well, you can't avoid the fact Socialism is an ideology.

I think there has opened a gap between those who were confronted by the real and threatening dragon of Nazism, out to destroy them, and those who have come after and whose tut-tutting is of quite a different nature, happy to believe it is all finished and done with. It is simply ignored, like every other lesson of history, because thank goodness it no longer applies today. With universal ideological thinking unacknowledged, the developments on the same lines are inbuilt. In time they will come round again just as before. Is it not starting already in California?

It may not be a Corporal Schickelgruber next time. Islam seems to be sheltering a number of ideological terrorisms, and has been ever since the Caliphate seized control after the Prophet's death. The Kalifa claimed he was the "Follower" of the Prophet, but actually in ancient Aramaic Khali-phai does not mean "Follower" at all. It means precisely what it says: Khali-Phai, Khali-worshiping or Khali-worshiper.

Khali was the prehistoric Black Goddess of the night, the goddess of death and destruction, of deceit and all deeds of the dark, worshiped from prehistoric times by the Qureishi tribe of Mecca, because when a meteor struck Aden, forming the crater, (A-den in Ancient Aramaic is "That-Hole" or "The-hole", in which the ancient city was built, as the mound of earth thrown up by the impact was shelter from the sun. The heat of the impact formed masses of shards of glass from the sand, which can be collected from the mound – but you would be ill advised to visit Yemen today, unless you are a jihadi. The formation of the crater had no political significance. Oil leaked to the Surface and caught fire; the rocks north of Aden are all burned black. It was many thousands of years ago, nobody has any idea how many, because so far as we know it had no connection with the end of the last Ice Age which ended about ten thousand years ago, when the seas rose 160 feet world wide.

The meteor was travelling north to south and the whole of Arabia and the Reed Sea was spattered with meteorites from the meteor's tail. One small black meteorite landed at Mecca. It was larger than a golf ball, but smaller than a tennis ball, made of black Flint. It did no harm and it left a clearly marked splash where it had gone in the ground. In Ancient Aramaic, hardly known these days since the Arabs all changed to Arabic, "Mecca" is from Mai-ka, Mai is "Fall of", and ka was "strike, hard, hard place, the place", so Mecca is "The place of the fall" and the Quereishis dug it out; and since it was of black flint they supposed it was a message from the Black Goddess Khali, sent down to them; and since it had arrived right beside them, finding a safe place to land without doing them any harm, they assumed it was an expression of protection and welcome and an offer to be their goddess and look after them. So they dug the meteorite out and built an enclosure round the splashmark, as holy ground, and named it the Ka'a'ba, from "Ka-a-ba" meaning "Place-that-it went" and in due course set the meteorite in the wall of the Ka'a'ba for worship.

It was Khali who offered any of her worshipers seven virgins in the hereafter who succeeded in killing fifteen non-believers in Her. The seven day week had just been introduced, we don't know when it was, or why, but it meant you got a new virgin every day of the week, and then round and round again for eternity. In Khali's day the next world was supposed to be much the same as this one, with just the nasty bits left out, so it was not unreasonable to think you might arrive in the next world with your wedding tackle intact.

But The Prophet Mohammad, just like the Prophet Jesus and all the Prophets of the Bible knew the next world was a spiritual one and there was no sex involved, so Osama bin Laden who promised his jihadis virgins was a heretic and worshiped Khali, whether he knew it himself or not, and deserved death as a genocide, and the same applies to the other jihadi bombers.

Much later than the Adeni meteor, thousands of years, The Prophet Mohammad occupied Mecca in a surprise night-time occupation and forgave all the Khali-phai, the Khali-worshipers, his brethren, who had for some forty years been trying to kill him, if they converted to Islam. But some of them only pretended, using the deception preached by the Goddess Khali; and after The Prophet's death formed the Khaliphai, which they claimed meant "Followers", when the original Aramaic was actually the reverse, it meant Khali worshipers and not Muslims at all.

Killing for Khali, all of them earning their seven virgins in the hereafter, they genocided all those who spoke Ancient Egyptian and refused to change to Arabic, destroying the Ancient Egyptian civilisation and then fighting their way all along the North African coast genociding the populations, and into Spain – all in the name of Islam, which means Mercy. The jihadism of Osama bin Laden, ISIS, and the other jihadi movements sheltered by Islam around the world are heretical. These are all fraudulent ideologies which need exposing for the irrationality in their supposed rationality. What is more the jihadis are all originally from the Quereishi tribe of Mecca who in pre-historic times worshiped the Black Goddess Khali, the goddess of death, destruction and deceit. Full stop. In those far off days I am afraid virtually everyone was a mentally lazy ignoramus with little understanding.

After the meteorite fell at Mecca, many thousands of years ago, the Qureishi tribe were soon taking on their mission to rid the world of Unbelievers-in-Khali and their neighbouring tribes found their villages getting raided for fifteen bodies at a time. Every Quereishi needed fifteen bodies, no less, in order to secure his reward of virgins for eternity. The Qureishi acquired the sobriquet of Wahabi. It means terrorists in ancient Aramaic: Wa-ha-bai, Terror, rejoicing-in, in being: i.e. Lifetime terrorists. At the time they were proud of it, and since those old days they have forgotten what it meant; so the Saudi King is still proud to be a Wahabi because it goes back to so long ago, but he is not a terrorist and expels any he finds. However it appears he can sometimes have somebody killed, if he displeases him. Primitive kings are like that. Going back a long way gives people self-confidence; but actually of course everyone goes back as far, or they would not be here today.

It is arguable the Quereishi were in Arabia even before the Akkadians came down from Lake Van to Arabia for Grass to feed their goats, over five thousand years ago. If that is so, the Arabs are not the same Semites as the Jews, which perhaps explains why they fight so.

We know now why the Jews cut off their foreskins, (actually copying the Egyptian Pharaoh, who was not a Pa-rao as Sir Wallis Budge thought in 1921 (when he published his dictionary, much of it wrong) was a royal roof or in other words the Royal House but actually a Pa-hai-rau or Penis Royal, i.e. divine, (so his sexual performance was critical for the well-being of all Egyptians), and he wanted his foreskin, which he thought was a muzzle cover, cut off so he could fire first and not have to wait for the supposed female vaginal rays to peel it back for him, (which he knew he did not do himself because it was not a muscular action, but engorgement with his blood which he did not feel), so he believed his erection and libidinousness was rayed into him with a ray from the opposite sex. The Egyptian rays, which the Ancient Egyptians copied from this mistaken sexuality, quite likely all humanity's mistaken sexuality at the time, were numerous, including those from the sun god Ra which the Egyptian priests drew with hands on the end so Hodge would understand it was they which were pulling the plants up towards the sun on their return journey back up to their source: all these Egyptian rays were radar style rays, there and back, accounting for all action at a distance, including the vision of the eye, little ra. The Pharaohs started it, and the Jews copied, and finally stuck a copy foreskin made of cloth on the back of their heads as well, in this case to stop bad thoughts getting in, round the back. (Of course neither removing the foreskin or sticking an artificial one on the back of the head ever made or makes any difference but nobody has noticed so far. They keep at it). We do not know why the Arabs cut off their foreskins but do not try to stop bad thoughts getting in at the back of their heads. Do they know? Could it be because Khali liked the idea of a passage for evil thoughts at the back of the head? The Pope keeps his foreskin on but tries to keep bad thoughts out round the back of his head, as well as wearing a Pharaoh's head dress. We do not know about Dr. Welby's foreskin, but we know he relies on his own initiative to control his thinking, and does not try to keep bad thoughts out round the back of his head, so I will guess his genitalia are in mint condition too.

He only allows two sexes, as well, the male and female, none of this ideological jumble of imaginary genders invented by LGBT(Q), which humanity can not possibly accommodate socially; so they will have to go, in spite of the ideology which has been conjured up in support of Stonewall's plethora of absurdities. It is simply ideological illusion with all the ferocity and absurdity of ideological thinking, a classic case in fact, to be put alongside Hitler's Nazi ideology, with no reality whatever, as the two strongest cases of ideological thinking so far. There may be any number of folk who hanker after a different sex to the one they were born with, but they can not acquire a sex change at whim, or indeed at all. It just can not happen. Nature can not do it, and it is quite beyond surgery. Even a simulacrum is unpersuasive. The more absurdity promoted by ideologists the more folk will want to join the ideology, that is how ideological thinking works. They cluster for mutual support and cling to their own idiocy.

There is now a scientific paper from scientists in Holland that demonstrates hormones used to support sexual transformation to suit those who think their gender is different from their sex is actually killing them sooner than sober males and females who are not so injected. This is one of the most tiresome ideologies, along with

Cancel Culture, which is as troublesome because it is so all-inclusive. Neither of them can survive the identification of the illusory nature of our ideological thinking for the last four hundred thousand years which is in this book, which comes from scientific Linguistics research. An omnium clean-up is required. Nothing is beyond challenge. If it follows the pattern of ideological thinking it is illusion. If it is defended with extreme animosity it confirms its illusionary nature. Hitler's Nazi ideology is a similar classic.

Hitler was of course a Marxist too. That is probably where he picked up his ideological thinking. That is why I have taken on the demolition of Marx's thinking as a priority. It does not mean Victorian entrepreneurs were better (or worse) than they were. It just means Marx's thinking was ideological, absurd, and should be dismissed. It is not as if anybody before had spotted that much. Now we know why. The political parties involved worldwide are just going to have to sort themselves out. They have to face up to the universal falsity of ideological thinking by all of us, which inevitably includes them. They can not just exclude themselves!

All religions and all sciences involve ideological thinking too. Philosophers, all wed to ideological thinking, are fewer these days. But Professor Sarah Brodie, 1941 to 2021, whose life was spent lecturing and writing about Aristotle in universities in Scotland, England and America, had an obituary in the Telegraph on 30 August 2021, which is how I got to know about her life work. She was thinking ideologically. Her obituary said: "Charming, unaffectedly stylish and kindly, she occasionally cut a forbidding figure, particularly when matters of scholarly standards were at issue. [She was thinking blatantly ideologically, just like Aristotle before her]. Manifestations of pretention or vacuity [Un-Aristotelian thinking] were liable to be met with sharp and unmistakeable correction, or silence and a quiet and paralysing stare." I had not heard of her. Her thinking can safely be identified as ideological. One wonders if she ever addressed the fact Aristotle believed women were mortal and only men could look forward to an after-life. The ladies joined their cousins the slugs. Ideological thinking can accommodate distinctions to taste, and Aristotle's, admittedly some time ago now, most people today will surely feel was fundamentally misogynistic. I guess Professor Brodie remained in her prime belief Aristotle was impeccable, and was quite unaware of the error of the ideological thinking we are all apt to adopt and the grave error it leads us all into.

It does appear some Professors seek their professorships to armour plate their thinking with academe so they can preach it and teach it. Quite similarly, the violence of the Taliban and jihadis is a pointer to their ideological thinking, theirs carried forward from prehistoric times without any break or consideration in ten thousand years or more. This is the source of the Wahabi pride. Ignorance is the only possible explanation. But then ignorance is common enough, along with the ideological thinking which goes with it. Duchess Meghan delights me: she makes me feel my years stuck in linguistics has all been well worthwhile. She has resurrected Herbert Marcuse, a 1930s German Marxist, effectively a Nazi thinker, who concluded there is no objective reality so we can and should all make up our own truth, whilst nevertheless giving it the credibility due to the commoner universal truth all the rest of us believe in. She is not a German historian so she must have picked it up from Antifa in California, who no doubt had adopted it some years before for the same purpose as the Duchess: so they could make up falsity as truth in accordance with their ideological thinking, which welcomes falsity. She actually declared this ideology on TV, immediately followed by her personal drivel as if it were sane thinking. Her education appears to be a Californian one, and California is a nest of woke ideologies and the latest home of the Democratic Party in the USA, and so the spiritual home of an old American President with a slipping brain. What a mess!

They all need to read my book and get around to sorting their ideological thinking out. They are wedded to falsity, and it does rather stick out by now. That does not mean I therefore must welcome everything about Mr Trump, but it is true I worked for Brexit with Mr Farage, though he did all the work. I was just able to brief him from my personal knowledge that the EU is not democratic but is a Nazi conspiracy by the French and German Presidents in 1950, both still secretly lost in Nazi ideology, to introduce into the European Coal and Steel Community Treaty in their negotiation of the terms in the Quai d'Orsay in Paris in 1950 secret codicils establishing Hitler's post war "Thousand Year European Fourth Reich". The EU has had the constitution written by Dr. Goebbels in 1943 for Hitler's post war European Fourth Reich ever since 1951.

The important truth is we have all been thinking in ideological terms for 400,000 years. It is almost a miracle we have got as far as we have, nearly all of us pumping in our vehement falsity with our unconscious ideological thinking. I have estimated elsewhere our universal ideology has been responsible for delaying the progress of human thinking by probably as much as some hundred and fifty thousand years, or even more, since we began to speak, (and think much). It is Scientia, the preparedness to reject what does not fit the actual facts as mistaken, which has done it. But that just makes the ideologist even crosser. We ought to be hearing loud and clear from the scientists, but it is possible to make an ideology even out of science itself, a scientism, in disregard of reality, with ideological thinking purporting to be scientific.

David Leeming's 2015 "Oxford Companion to World Mythology", a 469 page hardback, finds thousands of mythologies and fearlessly includes all religions, comparing their God-Man heroes and heroines, regardless of their truth values (i.e. counting as the same mythical thinking whether true or not). He has listed thousands, including the (later) version of Kali or the Indian Great Goddess Devi in her avatar as the wife of Shiva, the Destroyer. But Leeming's interpretations of his myths are quite unreliable. His Islamic myths include the Ka'aba ("the place that it went", {where Khali's black meteorite went} in primitive Aramaic, perhaps ten thousand years ago) which he describes as meaning "the cube", the modern building's present shape, and so on; no doubt served up to him by some ignorant devotee, perhaps even to promote some kind of "Cubist" thinking, whatever that might be. Moreover he has no idea of the universal ideological thinking of humankind which is what fires up his mythologies. There have been 400,000 years of Lemmings, all unawares. Even when they have picked up the ideology they have not recognised it as such. But, so far as he is concerned, his myths are just mistakes, not ideological addictions.

Yet he creates a splendid list of mythologies, so his book is a list of thousands of ideologies, and it can now surely be seen they are even better described as ideologies than mythologies, with divorce from any reality in this world, but absolute conviction of a story line picked for other purposes which had its appeal for the thinkers involved, and these of course vary widely with history. Had he known of humankind's universal addiction to ideological thinking he would have had no difficulty accepting it and relating mythology to ideology. Indeed it is surprising confirmation of how easy it is to indulge in ideological thinking and yet be totally unaware of it, for ever and a day – well anyway for the first 400,000 years since we first spoke.

It can I think be seen now that Marx's Das Kapital, which I spent some time on above (because it is still widely regarded as the classic ideological work supporting ideological thinking) - was something of an after-thought - a forty year after-thought. It is perfectly possible only a dozen people ever read it. It was forty years too late to have any news value. I think he wrote it as a stopper, to stop any contradiction. It was the Communist Manifesto which alone spread Communism, and after all what is a manifesto? It exemplifies what is manifest, plain or obvious, so that no particular evidence is required; and certainly none is offered in the 60 pages which sketch how it could and should now be done. Communists, who had decided it would be good, thought the proletariats in the leading economies would think the same and be the first to manifest the same thinking and arise and seize power; but they weren't. They assessed the improvements to their health, wealth, living conditions (accommodation and nutrition) and prospects of this new mechanical industry as too positive and encouraging to risk for a chance of something better which was quite uncertain and could easily turn out not as good. They were the sane ones and look how right they have proved. Marx was quite mad by comparison. It was the proletariats in the tyrannical economies with savage rulers who rebelled, it was those rebellions which miscarried and finished in other tyrannies, little if any better off. They were originally savage and communism led to more savagery, to be brutally frank. Everyone can now see liberal rule is preferable, so that tyranny is needed to stop people choosing it, and that was communism precisely. Liberalism is even more preferable if the regime has captured many of their citizens and forced them to conform. Beijing Emperors even sent their armies south in winter to castrate all the boys in their colonial provinces they could catch up, forcing those who valued their sex and were quick enough, to flee abroad. That is why there are all the Overseas Chinese today. The girls followed them wanting babies, and only northern Mongol ones were available within China at the time as the colonial boys remaining were no longer fertile. The emperors were all genocidal tyrants. Mao was no better. He was happy killing girls by only allowing one child (a boy to look after his parents). So girl babies just had to be secretly killed, so the parents could have another chance of care in their old age. Does anyone think Mao did not know what was going on? They should read Dr, Li's book. Of course he knew. He thought it was well worthwhile for the inestimable benefits of the community communism was inexorably working towards. That was and is Chinese Communism precisely, inscrutable, inhuman, cruel, power-hungry at all costs, mad, vile, disastrous, amongst other things not thinking about environmental factors which do not enable communism, a classic ideological addiction, quite out of rational control.

The fact is Communism was carried around the world by the 60 page handbook the 1824 "Communist Manifesto" written by Karl Marx and Friedrich Engels together. Engels was a businessman and not a thinker or philosopher. In those days the two professions were as different as chalk from cheese. The Manifesto was relatively short and simple: even Mao, who was not bright, had read it. There was no question of him reading Capital. He had some English but he did not care for science, it was too complicated, and Marx's philosophy was far far worse. There were Russian Communist emissaries in Djakarta by the middle of the century, encouraging the Indonesians to pick up Communism, and they just had the sixty page

Manifesto too. It was the English edition. But it was simply premature. There wasn't enough industrialisation in Indonesia to understand what it was talking about. China was little better, for that matter. China had British trains, which were starting to pull the country together, and the railway staff did try striking for better pay, but they were a tiny proportion of the population and were ignored. Incidentally railways, introduced to India by the British East India Company, which actually transformed India into a single country, formerly a congeries of warring statelets, Hindu and Muslim, with a powerless nominal Muslim Emperor, these trains are now targeted as a form of "slavery" by woke ideologies. They were in reality the opposite, a champion of advancement and administrative and industrial progress, even a splendid symbol of freedom and progress, and yes, even civilisation. Relating them to "slavery" is a classic intellectual perversity which all ideological thinking involves and all ideologists have no difficulty adopting. All ideological thinking is vulnerable to a sense of this kind of mischief. It effectively says "and while we are about it (amending the thinking) let's do it thoroughly and contradict all that we don't like, what was introduced by the intruder, the oppressor. But the oppressor actually advanced the country a hundred ways and admittedly still left it behind. The natives had obviously been doing a lot worse. Nobody is asking countries colonised to recognise as much. They should just forget it all and make their way forward now on their own, as best they can. Imperialists always knew they would not be thanked for improvements made. Politicians never give thanks, they just seek justification; and the first step is always to blackguard the opposition.

Britain was all one religion. Colonies were disastrous mixes. It handicapped them all. In colonial lands there were two or more ideological elephants in the same room. That's it really. So why sulk?

The Communist Manifesto was very simple. It simply said now is the time to introduce Communism, a national reorganisation of everything, by way of revolution, in order to improve efficiency. There was no argument. It declared communist society an ideal society, which would obviously be the most efficient. All disputes and oppression would disappear. But apart from in Europe it really wasn't yet time. Industry was needed, not too little but also not too much. In Europe there was too much so the workers, who were astonished by the increase in their wages and living standards, (just as Marx was too, and says so in Das Capital), and they were (unlike Marx) generally not too keen to start pulling it all to bits for something proposed as going to be so much better. Communists expected the most developed economies would prove to have the proletariats which would be the first to rise up. In practice it worked the other way about. Russia was backward and badly administered, but agitators from Europe were available. A magical improvement was badly needed. So Russia started it all, and Stalin lasted longest. China was even more backward and ill administered than Russia and the only agitators they had were complete learners like Mao. His ideology was without any independent thinking. He had spent years studying, but his studies were worthless. His thinking was confined to his ideology, and all that he had was out of The Communist Manifesto, which had no arguments, it just said have a go now. There wasn't any thinking any better around in China at the time. Emperors were only concerned with disciplining their southern provinces captured in their imperial centuries and their own mandarins, ministers, spent forty years learning and developing the Mandarin language fully. It was too difficult for the Chinese population, who were therefore only semi articulate. The southern provinces comprising Beijing's captured empire spoke their own languages, not Mandarin.

So Mao's ideological belief was without relief of any sort. As he got further and further out of his depth intellectually over the years his ideological thinking came to amount to insanity, as his personal Chinese but American educated doctor, Dr. Li, reported of him after his death – Li just had not spotted his thinking was ideological, he did not know about that. Mao killed more than the emperors from starvation, never mind those he put down with his proactive policy for eliminating illicit thinking, (all that was outside his own ideological beliefs) as well.

Eventually China acquired its modern achievements chiefly from the Overseas Chinese who had acquired their financial know-how indirectly from Hong Kong, which of course was a British colony and an advertisement for capitalism, which in reality was the opposite of slavery and the route to enlightenment; and it was the overseas Chinese who flocked to Hong Kong along with the unemployed from China itself, and started the intensive industrialisation, first within Hong Kong itself, but then also in Quantung (or Quandong) Province, just over the border from the Hong Kong New Territories, which the overseas entrepreneurs, now established in Hong Kong, proceeded to colonise from the little railway station on the Hong Kong border. I was guarding the border as an artillery observer at the time, in 1953. We had twelve 25 pounder field guns, and three battalions, about two thousand men in all to oppose however many armies the Chinese cared to throw at us. The capitalist industry which these overseas Chinese entrepreneurs took over the border from Hong Kong on the little railway – Hong Kong had no more land it could spare from paddi for food - was so popular with the peasantry of Quantung (who found themselves handed a living with a full diet for the first time), that

Peking did not care to challenge the development of the province from Hong Kong by the Overseas Chinese entrepreneurs, although their capitalism was contrary to their policy, which wanted the overseas Chinese overseas, as hostile and divergent thinkers, many speaking Cantonese like the population of Quantung.

One third of the Chinese Gross Domestic Product, GDP, is now the industry the Overseas Chinese have by now developed within China. They have built whole giant new industrial cities along the east coast of China. Beijing does not trust them. But they have no census to tell who comes from overseas. These are now intelligent, educated Mandarin speaking overseas Chinese, indistinguishable from permanent Chinese residents, except perhaps by their industrial initiative. Hong Kong was a little London so far as the Overseas Chinese were concerned. It started them off a hundred years before their competitors as the entrepreneurs in London started the British industrial revolution off a hundred years before the countries of mainland Europe in the previous century.

The overseas Chinese, who fled the southern colonial half of China when the Emperors were sending their armies south in winter in the sixteenth century, to castrate any boys they could catch in the villages, in order to keep their colonies placid, are known to want to give the Beijing Mongols a riposte when they can. But Beijing has the army. Still, it might change sides one day. I think it will. All humans like liberal democracy best because with liberal democracy life is best. It is that simple. You might think tyranny would be best because that way you could take from those the tyranny tyranises but it doesn't work out because being under a tyranny is always uncomfortable. Tyrannical people are bad by nature.

Financial mismanagement from Western manipulation of economic terms is about the only weapon we have at present with President Zhi's Belt and Road, but there is the Overseas potential. Even the English that two hundred and fifty million Chinese boys and girls are now learning is actually a threat to Communism, because it caters for so much more; and the invasion of English and American universities by relatively wealthy Chinese students is a threat in the long term. Some of them are bound to notice, they aren't stupid, and rejoice in education, which has only recently been available for most of the Chinese population. There are now many proletarian Chinese brighter than Mao ever was. His parents were farmers, their farm was 3 acres, a patch not viable in the west (unless with truffle trees). Mao worked on it as a boy. The family ran it, they employed nobody. His Mandarin was comparatively limited.

Now the Communist Manifesto was a 60 page pocket book, a declaration it is time for the communisation of society, by way of revolution and the massacre of the opposition, everyone but the proletariat. Lenin may have read the first German edition of Das Kapital. Stalin didn't. There wasn't a Russian edition. The Russian agitators sent to Indonesia were ignored. They had the 60 page Manifesto, that was all. The two Russians who arrived in China in 1820 were not appreciated. They spoke Mandarin they had learned from the Chinese in France, but not well. They judged the working class in China too backward to campaign for communism on their own, and advised they should start by collaborating with the bourgeoisie in order to build up industry, before turning on them later. This did not suit the few Chinese members of Communist parties in any of the provinces, who felt it demeaned their abilities. It did of course, but the advice was sound. The Russians were soon left out of talks. Mao felt the purity of the original Communist ideology should not be tampered with. Mao's father was a comparatively well off farmer, (his family were fed) but his farm was only three acres, little more than a cottage garden here, and the family provided the labour needed to grow crops to feed the family and sell a surplus to buy other goods, clothes and shoes. Mao had worked on the farm as a young child, a family duty. The Chinese planned to influence the soldiers in the militias of the war lords to get them to become communists, as the industrial proletariat was thin on the ground.

After the long march, when Sun Yat Sen was gone, and Mao was Chairman, the Communist Party wrote its own analyses. In typical ideological fashion, the truth has not been allowed to challenge the ideology. The ideology is the only truth, however much it departs from the reality. In China, millions starved. After Mao's death, his personal doctor who had been his only companion, discovered the party planned to have him killed, because he was a threat to their version of the facts if they needed to change them for any reason later, so he fled to America and rewrote the 500 pages in Mandarin he had been obliged to burn by the party, and it is translated into English and now records Chairman Mao's gradual descent from ideology to insanity. It happens. Hitler was the same, on drugs for the last year and more, which is why his assassination was attempted, not just because he was Nazi, but because by then he was crazy too. Stalin finished up killing traitors he imagined betraying the communist ideology; he judged them intuitively and tipped off Comrade General Bobkin to have them killed. That was effective insanity. Bobkin too! It is the very model of a modern ideologist; and we all think ideologically, even when it has not reduced us to this degree of insanity. The inability to see outside our ideologies is universal, and has been since we first spoke. It is Scientific Linguistics which has cracked this nut and provided the first complete description of ideological thinking which gives us the opportunity to see through the fraudulence involved in all ideological thinking. Every politician needs to know this, and to understand the significance, in order to climb out of the pit of ideological misunderstanding we have been confined in for the last four hundred thousand years. Ideological thinking is messing us all up, particularly those making the ideologies up and then confined to them. So you can see it can be easily overlooked.

In this chapter I include examples from the daily newspapers of ideological thinking which makes the news on a daily basis, to show how ideology influences our thinking. Every day there are examples of the absurdity of ideology and its departure from reality, as well as the vehement and violent response to any challenge of any ideology and the absurd behaviour it produces. I have for some days now cut out the texts from the Daily Telegraph and put them in order. It takes quite a time, and the staff of the Daily Telegraph, a conservative UK paper, are now inclined to feature them all, or mostly on the same page, which shows they are aware of the commonality of the thinking, and yet they are apparently quite unaware of the universality of ideological thinking and the inevitable misconceptions, absurdity, viciousness and violence it involves. These are daily revisitations of Adolf Hitler's mischiefs, we are all required to tolerate, with not one of those responsible in the least degree aware of the fraudulence and maliciousness of their thinking. There has to be a major campaign of cleansing of the stables. World leaders are all included in the ideological thinking, which is what currently renders the world so disgusting, in spite of the technological improvements. Some may not have the brains to follow the analysis of the falsity of the Marxist dialectic in my linguistics books, and in my chapter 2 here. Certainly all the woke ideologies coming today out of California in the United States are also Marxist ideologies and they all think in dialectical terms although the dialectic is simply erroneous, confusing two lines, the ordinary boundary line which, inter alia, encloses a category and the continuum, which can be represented as a similar line, but isn't. The continuum was not recognised until Bertrand Russell, the distinguished mathematical thinker, pointed it out; and Marx had been basking in the dialectic he had from the eighteenth century German philosopher, Emanuel Kant, which Marx had actually misidentified as the work of Georg Hegel, another German philosopher a generation later, on which he thought he was basing his own understanding for Das Kapital (as he said standing Hegel on his head, with a materialist philosophy in place of an idealist/intellectual one). You can have an ideology with materialist implications, but rather more dubiously a materialist philosophy, since a philosophy is entirely a mental composition, the result of human thinking, a mental state of affairs, and not a methodology, which might be in terms treated as materialist.

Anyway philosophy is out now, apart from logic. The latest science of Linguistics has taken over the philosophical area of debate, along with some of the area of psychology.

I start my newspaper references to the ideological cases each day in the UK Daily Telegraph, a conservative daily, on 23 October 2021. Batter has replaced batsman in the laws of cricket.

Actually man here is used genderless, mankind, it is an operative, the equivalent of the -er in batter. But everything now is to be re-evaluated in terms of ideological thinking. LGBTQ has an influence, they will be thinking some batters will in future be trans girls, that is males who have picked a feminine gender, though still with their full male genitalia, so wouldn't care to be taken as male, although they are. It is an example of how Human Relations are taking over the thinking of the western world. At the same time we learn that the Education Secretary is drawing up new guidance for schools to understand their duties when it comes to teaching controversial materials: in short "White Privilege" should not be taught as a fact when it is only a theory. Of course if you are trying to get an ideology accepted as a fact, because you believe them all, you naturally tend to record them as fact.

The next day, 24 October, yields no less than seven cases of ideological thinking. In Vienna, Museums are putting copies of naked statues and paintings on pornographic websites to punch back at prudish social networking posts. Woke ideology seems to be a bit different in Vienna.

But in the UK the National Trust Annual General Meeting next week anticipates newly formed groups of rebel attacks on its blatant woke policies condemning the original owners of many of the houses they are supposed to be looking after, with notices about disgraceful conduct they have dug up stuck up in the buildings.

Also, Lionel Shriver, a critic, has said authors may stop writing historical fiction for fear of not being sufficiently censorious where woke ideology requires it, and suffering abuse.

The Pitt Rivers Museum in Oxford is hiring a curator at £9,000 pa to examine 2800 human specimens to see if they are obliged to return them. The judgment of Solomon will be required as many are recorded as simply African.

Malcolm Morley, the Vice President of the British Veterinary Association, has said the BVA has questioned 18,000 members in the UK and 15% have experienced discrimination in their work place or learning environment this year, and some of the conversations with colleagues may be difficult, so will members please refrain from complimenting the work of white vets.

Meanwhile many top schools' History and English lessons have been swiftly adapted to be more "global", after students complained they were too White, Male and Eurocentric.

A leading head teacher, Victoria Bingham, has now said adult teachers should not crumble as educators as the first woke student agitators want. Apparently they have! Well some are woke too, but Ms. Bingham does not mention that.

Finally to cap it all, academic John McWhorter has a page with Zoe Strimpel in which he insists that Wokism is itself racist and he seeks to highlight the absurdities of America's new religion. He means their ideologies, of course. Apart from these seven informative articles the rest of the newspaper is concerned with domestic affairs or democracy.

There were fourteen days of this, over five pages, which somehow got taken out, I don't know how; and I can't recover the newspapers to put them back in; and anyway I believe by now virtually every one else must be noticing it too, so why bother. It all delays publication.

I might however restore the pagination to some extent by adding in here, to take the place of the missing days of ideological news with a note on the road rage which has even led to drivers actually killing the drivers offending them after getting out of their cars. It never used to be like this. Of course speeds have got faster, trips have got longer, and evidently tempers shorter – and there are these smart motorways too, which whatever else they provide add to the tempo of driving on them. It seems clear drivers today are apt to be pressured into adopting ideological thinking as they drive by all or any of this. The offensive driver is not thinking right, he is outside the ideology – so of course he deserves a violent response, and can be killed in the Street just like Dr. Andy Ngo for challenging the ideology. The killer doesn't back out of his mouse trap. There will be cases where other murderers have been guilty of their own ideological thinking, perhaps even all of them. We often hear their thinking was noticeably awry.

The Nazi ideology has been installed all across Europe by the European Union for the last seventy two years, since the negotiation of the European Coal and Steel Community Treaty was hijacked by the French and German Presidents in 1950, who were still secretly Nazi; and the European Union constitution since 1951 has been the one written by Dr. Goebbels in 1943 for Hitler's post-war "Thousand Year European Fourth Reich", which was copied from the Nazi archive in Berlin and sent to the European Commission in Brussels run by the joint dictators of Europe, the French and German Presidents, by the German war criminals imprisoned by the international court at Nuremberg in 1945 when they were all released by the USA in 1951, preliminary to the USA insisting on re-establishing NAZI Germany immediately thereafter, as a bulwark against Soviet Russian Communism in the Cold War. Another copy has been taken by the chair of the CIB (Campaign for an Independent Britain) in the UK since, Edward Spalton, a German speaker, who also read the Nazi archive in Berlin; and it is word-for-word the same as the European constitution. The Commission installed it as the European constitution immediately in 1951 without consulting any European countries, and it has been hidden in plain sight for over seventy years since; which is strong evidence of the power of ideological thinking to traduce the truth when they are in conflict. It is also evidence of the close cousinship of European Socialism and Hitler's National Socialism, in so far as the 26 European nations subscribing to the constitution of the European Union have all been content for over seventy years now to be governed by Nazis, whilst at the same time back paddling furiously to establish Hitler's National Socialism, a Marxist party, (that is what Nazi spells) was really a far right party, to give them a bit of space between Hitler's holocaust and European Socialism. Nazism is the party of fraudulent lies, and the EU is the union of fraudsters. Today fraud is universal in Europe. The majority of politicians, (who are Remainers), in the UK are either ignorant or fraudulent too. It is polite to regard them mostly as ignorant. But then they have to be ideologists to stay ignorant in face of the truth, and this can often be shown to be the case. Legal ideologies are often responsible. The High Court nurtures Nazi-Europe lovers, because European law was sent to them before parliament so they dominated politics, the Nazi fraud exactly. But they could not see it because of their ideological thinking. They just thought it was good for them as their beliefs are tops.

As a final subject matter I am aware I ought to undertake an examination of the ideological thinking involved in the sexual phantasmagoria which has been put together by the LGBTQ lobby, led by the Stonewall Group in the UK. Sex is, of course, an area where strong emotional involvement arises, and rape and murder are both encountered when thinking goes wrong. The malign effects of ideological thinking are however universal. That is why they are to be found in this sensitive area even more powerfully than in any other area; and that is why the exposure of universal ideology can not leave sex out. It can indeed be regarded as the kernel of the case for reforming ideological thinking, that and Wokism equally, the two most outrageous deceptions today. It is sad to have to be as blunt as this, but the world is equally threatened by these two most outrageous ideologies, both of which must be challenged before they get any more indoctrinated. One is a political fraud, the other a domestic one. Neither is tolerable for anyone who has the slightest regard for the recognition of reality. I have respect for what Ludwig Wittgenstein would have recognised as "the case". I am in no way concerned with the sexual practices of the some one hundred and two different genders supposedly lurking within the pair of sexually different physical bodies which humanity has been content to tolerate as our inevitable endowment for ever, up until now. Homosexuality as well as Lesbianism are well recorded throughout history as long as we know it. It is a psychological issue, influenced by social norms. The distinguished classical historian who wrote "The Decline and Fall of the Roman Empire" in the nineteenth century was inclined to attribute both to the outbreak at the time of widespread homosexuality in Rome. The law in England condemned homosexuality at the time that he wrote, which may have encouraged him to pick on it as the cause of moral decline. It showed how bad it is. Around the same time the son of a member of the Upper House of Parliament was convicted of homosexual practices with Oscar Wilde, who was imprisoned.

When I was at Oxford University as an undergraduate, after war service in World War Two, in 1947, academia was a nest of homosexuals, led by the leading professor at All Souls College who was supposed to know most about William Shakespeare, the playwright. Nominally, homosexuality was still illegal, but nothing was done about it. The homosexual fraternity looked after each other. They can be said to have ganged up together. A history undergraduate who was a friend of mine, and homosexual, rubbed his leg up against mine, but I said "No thank you", with the "thank" emphasised to show that I was completely straight. In those days that was OK. Nobody had ever thought of the possibility of there being more than two basic genders and just two divergent approaches, the homosexual and the lesbian.

I had had an unusual upbringing as I had been the only boy with three sisters and two female cousins three and four years older staying with us for three years while their parents were in India. My Cousin Ian, their father was a soldier, and overseas tours were then three years, time to learn the language and understand the country and its people. When I was eight these extra girls left and I was sent to boarding school, all boys; but when I got home at the end of my first term I found my mother had built a wing on the farmhouse and started a girl's school for what became sixty girls, and when our terms did not match I had the girls descend on my house before I left or found them still in occupation when I returned. These were not ordinary feeble girls like most in those days. They were being toughened up by riding horses every day. They did lessons too, in fact I think more than most, but still not all that much. None became professors.

It was a great success. There were many girls wanting to be toughened up. In the 1930s there were hardly any other activities for girls. We soon had an outdoor swimming pool with a bore with a pump, pumping in unheated water from 300 feet down; and four tennis courts. I may have only met them all for a few days at a time, but they all wanted to know me, because in those days even their brothers were kept pretty separate, and here was an opportunity to examine a boy, as my mother thought it would be good for them, as well as for me! So I just had to hold my nerve. I was their sole outlet, for investigating boydom. Sex was not an issue in so far as none of us knew anything about it. Some were the same age as my elder sister. My looks were hardly a draw; but they met no other boys. In summer I would swim in their pool with them. Younger girls just wore pants like me. I even rode their ponies too, but I would often fall off, I hadn't had any practice.

My sisters were intermediaries, so I got all the feminine gossip, whether I wanted it or not: "Now Jennifer has got a pash on Rosamund". (A pash was a passion, an emotional attachment. It wasn't regarded as sexual, because nothing was known about sex). There will have been some of them who thought babies came from under gooseberry bushes. A pash was just an urge to find somewhere private to talk together. From a comparatively early age these girls were all forming emotional attachments to each other, three or four years before any equivalent relationships at a boys' public school.

At public school, boys are maturing, and their sexual orientation is developing with puberty. They all start out with emotional responses towards younger boys, homosexual relations, whether they let them out or not; but I don't think in my time there was a case of any physical abuse. Boys were shy. If there was it was not discovered. Later in life of course this may be a very unwelcome memory and generally it is denied entirely, in fact it appears it is expunged entirely. Many men never even remember it happened. There is nothing unusual in any of this. Boys all enjoy the same activities, and anyway there is no choice. But unlike the girls, boys are intensely private at this stage, evidently aware it is not supposed to be. They will always lie if challenged. The difference is probably just because girls are younger when the emotion comes upon them, when social thinking is less developed. They emote without a thought. Generally, however, the objectivity of their attraction will shift slowly to the other sex, so it no longer occurs. It is when it doesn't that you got a homosexual or lesbian adult, a left-over from an intermediate stage of development. They haven't got different genes, they just haven't fully matured, for one reason or another.

The reasons for getting left over at an earlier sexual stage are various and hard to determine, suggesting they are frequently numerous and may cover a lot of different ground. They certainly aren't all the same. Alpha males don't get stuck. But feebler performers, at learning or playing, lose some in each generation who don't advance to full maturity, and instead either find a male partner or surrender to one. With same sex partnerships of this sort you get a simulation of a husband and wife emotional relationship. Unattached homosexuals however are usually pretty promiscuous and soon become infectious. That more or less sets the scene.

We now come to the fancy footwork involved in LBGTQ ideological thinking, which enables fantasists to make up their own reality more pleasing to them than the actual reality. I have already described their compositions as a fantasmagoria, with apparently a hundred and two different genders available for selection, and now we find something else. If you advertise an availability, you will find the spaces begin to be taken up, and at a younger and younger age. These are ideological spaces, and the simplicities of them have an ideological appeal, and once you have adopted a scheme of ideological thinking you are inclined to stay inside it. It would perhaps be unfair to describe an ideology as resembling a mousetrap; but it takes some perseverance and independence to dismiss the thinking you have adopted and embark instead in a new direction. Hitler never got out of his mouse trap.

Every member of Stonewall, the militant lobby group, which has master-minded the development of self-appointed genders to flout sexual identification and have males reidentified as if they were females, and vice-versa females as if they were males, have pursued the mission they have made up to an extent which amounts to so gross a departure from reality that I am afraid it may even become a form of insanity.

To assist in this sexual transmogrification, the language is to be altered, certain words banned, and others changed. As I have devoted much of my life by now to the study of historical etymology, the relationship of the semantics of language with its phonology, and the development of these patterns over the past four hundred thousand years since hominins began to speak, and for more time than the time that any one of these Stonewall worthies, who espouse the impossible, have fought to establish it, long after science has conclusively established it as falsity, I am unimpressed by their ideology. I can see the social problems from feeding a mix of sexes all into women's facilities. You can not do this without abandoning rationality. I am not accusing them of witchcraft, merely of an insouciance which provides them with a degree of negligence of reality which is probably no better. Yet I bear them no ill will. I have no interest in their sexual practices as such. I am not even interested in their psychology. But I do want our thinking to be rational. Ideology is not rational.

The malign effects upon those encouraged to undergo bogus sex changes, in pursuit of non-existent genders sought, should be legally compensatable in the courts, in so far as the wrong advice is in breach of our human rights. We are entitled to receive only true reports as to our medical treatment, and anyone who wantonly misadvises another person that assurances are well founded, when they plainly are not, should be treated as liable and punishable. The present position is politicians avoid confronting the issues at all and just let it run. Women are left to face the issues alone, left unsupported, just more victims of male chauvinism, as ever. Agitators threaten anyone writing the truth. A female professor is threatened with death, and unsupported by her university, undergraduates are not disciplined and left believing they have a right to dismiss any professor they disagree with (and apparently to even threaten her with death!) There is no doubt such undergraduates should be dismissed and made liable and punished for threats.

To refuse to concede a man is a man or a woman a woman in order to have them and cases of their trans or transformed sexes (a fraudulent transformation) described as if they were the same (when they are not) is to insist what is false is true, and amounts to deliberate deception for the satisfaction it provides, self-deception, or deception of third parties misadvised about the possibility of genders over-ruling the reality of sexual distinctions, which are part of the real furniture of the natural world, whereas these "genders" are just whimseys of human thinking.

Psychology is not a simple science, and ideological thinking is a confusion of human thinking. An ideologist must expect to make psychological errors. There is involved what used to be known as a category error. Human sexes are physical, biological, factual descriptions. They are real phenomena. You could describe them as part of the furniture of the universe, like any other physical phenomenon. This gender thinking is quite different, a human whimsey.

There is a literature now of books on sex and gender. These are, inter alia, Professor Stock's Book "Material Girls" which has got her into such trouble with the LGTBQ people. She is a Lesbian but has her head screwed on A modern "gender" is a completely different category to the two sexes. It is an idea, not a thing of any kind, because an idea is something we think of, and so it is included in someone's mind, or a plurality of them. But here is the point. A mind is an abstract term to describe all our mental activities or thoughts, our ideas. None of these have any physicality. A thought is a different category to any part of a physical body. A mind is no kind of thing, it is an abstract term for what we believe to be the activities of our brains. So don't go looking for a mind amongst phenomena, any more than the mileage of a motor car inside a motor car. It is not the same kind of category as a phenomenon, and to relate them as if they were the same is a category error, as you must, I am afraid, expect a professor of philosophy to spot. You certainly should not believe you are entitled to bully her into joining you in your absurd false thinking. Indeed as students you are not entitled to insist on your opinions. They are there to be tested, not promulgated.

As a matter of fact, we don't actually have much of an idea of the way thinking is related to the brain. We know a brain is alive and functions by way of electricity. But we have no idea how electrical activity in the brain is related in turn to an idea, and it certainly looks as if, while we have the brains that we have today, we never will.

We come out of this review briefed to reject any idea that thinking of a gender can alter any sexual phenomenon. It follows, as night follows day, (that is to say, as the rest of nature), that a transformed sex is an imaginary possession and can not be the same as a natural sex with which a body is born. Picking a gender different to a sex does not alter a sex, all it does is it just muddles the thinking. At this stage we are surely well advised to enquire why anyone would want to muddle up their thinking in the way that Stonehouse has been doing for many years now;

and the answer appears to be because they have been thinking ideologically. No surprise really, because we all have, ever since we first spoke. But it is now time to stop it. It can not be allowed to continue. Why? Because understanding about everything is lost if we just imagine the reality, when it is not the case, enshrining falsity in our ideological thinking. It is Meghan's philosophy, and as Harry does not query it I suppose his too. Herbert Marcuse was always wrong, he made up his philosophical beliefs, most philosophers, if not all of them, do if they rejoice in inventing schemes for people to adopt.

There is a literature on LGBTQ. I have read some of the books. There is "Material Girls" by Professor Kathleen Stock, who was professor of Analytical Philosophy at Sussex University. In the book she says she is a Lesbian, but the feminine sex is a birth condition and it has a material form. You may not care to take part in straight sex but you can not change your sex, it is quite firmly part of the furniture of the universe, obviously required for the continuation of the human race, just like the continuation of any other species.

For this book, and for her professorial lectures on philosophy as well, she is pursued with hatred and malice by a gaggle of undergraduates, (by definition, not as yet particularly well informed), who don't want what she says to be true, because it contradicts their ideologies, which I understand they have learned from a party of activists named Stonewall, because the ideologies suit them.

These ideologies, incidentally, have been implanted by intellectually unqualified teachers with sexual ideologies of one kind or another, starting on many of them as young children. This ideological infection has over the years spread into state schools, where some teachers are indoctrinated too.

The Sussex undergraduates raised a political agitation to have Professor Stock dismissed from her academic position at the university because they didn't like her ideas. Independent medical scientists rallied in her support, but university dons did nothing. University dons were in a quandary. They shouldn't have been. The Professor was thought to be in danger of assault; and the dons wanted students to have "safe space" so they can study without feeling threatened, and of course the students say in turn their safe space is threatened by these lessons which contradict their beliefs. They indeed do but it is their ideological thinking which is not right, not the philosophising; and if they are unable to tolerate correction they can not be taught and so they should be dismissed as mentally quite unfit for university study. It is not Professor Stock who is their problem, as they imagine, but actually intellectual education. It is not possible to have the bits you like but at the same time not other bits you don't like. Reason is not the same as unreason. You would think all university dons would recognise this at once. But no! Many are "woke". In short, they are labouring under ideological thinking and need correcting themselves before they can address the issues involved properly. What is more, this is not new. Magdalen College, at Oxford, has had ideological issues crop up in their Students' Common Rooms. Woke ideologies, which tend to attack former established thinking as outmoded, youth opposing experience, but at the same time novelty replacing remnants of previous times. Yes, times change, so we should expect it. But everything dreamed up is not an improvement on previous thinking, and it is ideological thinking which permits the false to burgeon at the expense of the true. With ideological thinking rampant, the world is back to front. The easy-goers go easy and the diligent are over-ruled. There are other books on LBGQ, a gaggle of which I have. There are many more. They approach these ideologies with other ideologies of their own. Nothing is learned. It is a burgeoning fuddlement.

Have we really been making ideological mistakes like this for four hundred thousand years?

Yes, we have. We really have. That is why we adopt ideological thinking so readily, and are so reluctant to set it aside. What is required, now we have discovered the nature of our mistakes up to now, is to establish the nature of an ideology (which I have tried to explain as best as I can in the next chapter) so that in future we can make our way past these traps without almost inevitably falling into them.

At present the fancy thinking of our ideologies is leading us all astray. Political life is fraud and deception. Every political party is at fault in every country, because of this faulty thinking. Members of parliament, all of whom are ideologists else they would have no reason to want to be MPs, labour under various misbeliefs, (some, of course, very much worse than others).

CHAPTER 4

THE IDENTIFICATION OF UNIVERSAL IDEOLOGICAL THINKING

This chapter is to identify the elephant in the room, ever since we first learned to speak: the universal inclination of mankind to adopt the ideological pattern of thinking so that we have all been misled, and have perverted our beliefs, which have all been wrong, and for the most part still are. It is an astonishing fact, indeed an almost unbelievable one, that for four hundred thousand years, ever since we learned to speak, we have been making this mistake and nobody has ever spotted it, our wretched brains have never revealed it. So we are still wed to it.

Linguistics is the newest science, the historical study of scientific linguistics, over the past fifteen years or so, which has led to this staggering identification, and I make no excuse for repeating what I have been saying over the course of the previous introductory chapters, and in my linguistics books over many years, so that the identifications I now need to compile can be properly headed. When I wrote my first book on the etymology of language, going back to the Stone Age, Linguistics was still in its original liberal arts format, and had been largely dominated by Noam Chomsky's ideological transformational grammar for about half a century, a philosophical scheme Chomsky (who was a Marxist undergraduate at MIT when he put his linguistic ideas together); and in those far off days the number of languages with their constitution and characteristics researched was far fewer than today, (say 10%). His transformations virtually had to cope only with the Indo-European family of languages, and their grammars were generally very similar anyway. He ignored the native American tongues entirely at the time, (which admittedly weren't much). That should have alerted him. His political extreme radicalism into old age must surely warn any intellectual examiner of the ideological nature of his thinking. He was a Marxist undergraduate when he dreamed up his ideological pattern of thinking to explain our grammatical achievements. He felt himself armour plated against contradiction by his belief in the Marxist dialectic; and now as he enters his nineties his Marxist political extremism is not one whit abated, although the dialectic Marx relies on is now demolished as a confusion of two lines, one the common or garden boundary line of the category and the other the continuum identified comparatively recently by Bertrand Russell, the distinguished mathematician, symbolic logician and grammarian. His understanding is altogether different. Anyone capable of swallowing Karl Marx's gibberish is an arch ideologist, they imagine the dialectic (thesis, antithesis, synthesis) guarantees their thinking is right, although it can now be shown to simply be a mistake. The mistake is to confuse a boundary line with a continuum. It is a simple intellectual error which can be seen once the difference between the ordinary straight line which surrounds every category is distinguished from the continuum, which Bertrand Russell identified. Until Russell, the distinction was not made, although once made it is obvious enough. That is ideological thinking for you.

So now here is what makes an ideology.

(1). All ideologists start out with an intellectual sense of grievance: with something missing which they feel is their due. You can of course pick up this feeling by going at it the other way about and adopting an outrageous belief so that there is a palpable rejection which you can then regard as a grievance. Woke ideologies are of this nature, but they are in any case all based on Marxism, so they all have Marx's ready-made grievance already, to get them started.

(2). There is usually on top of this the feeling that they have been robbed of their due, due to the malice of others. Nobody robbed Chomsky, he had adopted Karl Marx's sense of robbery of the working classes, which got him fuelled up, while still an (excessively opinionated) undergraduate. Hitler (Corporal Schickelgruber) had been robbed by the defeat of Germany in the first world war, which he believed was unwarranted. He went on, as we all know now, to identify Judaism as the malicious party which stole victory from Germany. He too was a Marxist, and could claim to be a German worker, and a remarkably intelligent one, since their education at the turn of the twentieth century was nothing much. Stalin's education was no better and his brains were a good deal worse. His robbery too was defeat in war, as well as the fighting in the revolution; and he came from Georgia, the least best province to come from (its virtue had been denied it. It was backward and uncivilised).

(3). All ideologists are affronted. They believe all those not sharing their ideology are criminals therefore and are properly punished. They will even punish a statue, believing it important work, and needing as many as possible to join in, for the feel-good factor derived. There is a distinct sense of mission, of importance out of the ordinary. It adds conviction that they are elite, dreaming all this up. It follows, of course, any shortfall in appreciation of the importance of your ideological thinking must be mischievous and damnable.

(4). An ideology provides you with such clarity of vision you are bound to be right, so anything which does not fit in with your ideology must be wrong. This makes all ideologies inward looking and quite unable to change their beliefs. This was in fact the purpose of the original ideological thinking when we needed an ideology to get us all thinking the same way so that we would all pick up the same meanings for the twenty four original phonemes as we learned to utter them, four hundred thousand years ago.

(5). It is essential to keep the ideology pure (correct, right), so your political beliefs are totalitarian. There is no room for any kind of uncertainty. This on its own means it is absurd.

(6). Your religious beliefs generally have no time for unbelievers. Although I have no doubt religious beliefs are ideological, just as scientific beliefs are too. I hesitate to include the major religions of the book because they are doing good, even if belief is sometimes wrong, (as I think I know it is bound to be).

I have however learned the first chapter of the Jewish Bible, Genesis, was borrowed (lock, stock and barrel) by the first Jewish tribe we know, the Akkadians, who were humble goatherds, after they came down from the hills north of Mesopotamia (now Iraq), around Lake Van, for better grass for their goats in Arabia, from their neighbours, the Sumerians, a much more civilised tribe (the Adamites) because the Akkadians admired what they felt to be the science in Genesis. The Sumerians, it is now known beyond a peradventure, had been driven out of Eastern Malaya about eight to ten thousand years ago when the last Ice Age melted, and the ice which had piled up on quite a lot of the land, apparently up to a mile high, as it would if it kept on raining or hailing or snowing, for an age. As a result Eastern Malaya, which stretched east from the present Malayan peninsular, the original hinterland, all the way to the Philippine Islands, a low lying flat pastureland with slow running rivers from west to east, which means Noah's flood came in from the East as the seas all round the world rose as the ice melted, eventually a hundred and sixty feet, measured in the South China Sea, where the Adamites lived and had built the first cities (well permanent villages, with skills and knowledge compared to the Akkadians). They had been able to feed themselves from paddy fields irrigated from the rivers through channels the women had dug from the rivers with their digging sticks for edible roots. This was Noah's flood, now for the first time a historical reality, before an obvious fantasy as we can all now see, because if the flood had taken place up in the hills, the scientific rules of water's behaviour provide only the mountain tops, like the Canary Islands, could have stuck out above the water. But then where could all the water have gone to when the dove came back to the ark with a twig in its mouth when all the water was abating. The Sumerians rebuilt their cities in Mesopotamia, whither Noah sailed. Noah means sailors in Sumerian. All the Sumerian records in Cuneiform writing, which the Sumerians had invented, have survived in the Sandy soil on clay tablets hardened by the sun and millions have been available for years, but interpreting them from scratch has been an enormous task and is still by no means complete. But there is, since 2014 enough known for a worthwhile dictionary of what is known to be published. (An earlier one was rudimentary). There are enough more clay tablets baked hard in the sun to keep translators going for lifetimes, if they are so inclined. A copy of the whole of Genesis in Sumerian cuneiform, earlier than the Akkadian Bible was written, has now been found. The correction of the mistakes in the Akkadian Bible makes it more believable, not less.

The Garden of Eden is a mistranslation of Eastern Malaya. A mali is a gardener in Sumerian as well as Malay, Sanskrit and Hindustani. Malaya means the Garden Land. It was not a flower garden. It refers to these first farming villages the Sumerians had made, probably with irrigated rice and cereals, and maybe vegetables too, there is no information. It must be remembered the early Greek cities some time later would today be described as villages too. Everything is much better understood as the original Sumerian language comes to light. It does rather put the cat amongst the pigeons for orthodox Judaism, because Adam, who had spoken with their God, it now transpires was not a Semite, and the God he spoke with was not the Jewish God even. Still, there is only one God. He would have been the same God worshiped by the

Sumerians. Judaism knows there is only one God and Adam spoke to him in Sumerian. There has been a movement to try and make out Sumerian was related to Akkadian so Adam can be recovered as a Semite. But it won't wash. They are not even of the same language family. But it does not affect the religion.

(7) An ideological belief usually has a competitive, or even a hierarchical element.

(8) You might think ideology requires a special kind of person, but it is actually the other way about. Ideology makes one.

The first ideology was devised, when first we spoke, to get everyone thinking the sounds we were learning to utter had meanings which were all the same for everyone. For this purpose it was argued the meanings of the twenty four phonemes (now meaningless letters of the alphabet retained to spell our sounds), had their 'natural' meanings, that is to say they had meanings echoic of the same sounds in nature. This was all very well, although strictly the sounds we were making in our throats weren't all that like what we were used to hearing in nature. So we were building false meanings into the system of language. This was required to get everyone thinking on the same lines, so we would all think of the same meanings for the sounds. So language and the presumptions which went to establish language were our first ideology: designed, as I say, as an essential presumption so we could all acquire the same meaning for each of the phonemes as we learned to utter them. We had no language to discuss the matter. The amazing thing is we were ever able to get everyone thinking the same at all.

I had spent 20 years working these original meanings out when I wrote my first Linguistics book. One of the most important sounds and meanings was ish (the sibilant). We thought it had the meaning of fire because when, at dawn, we dunked our burning brands (we kept burning at night to keep the sabre-toothed tigers at bay at the cave mouth) to save burning any more resin, (hard to find, on pine trees) they all said ishshsh as they went out and were gone. If they had said Rumpelstiltskin, quite likely Tarzan would have gone off in a sulk and we would have all stayed dumb for another four hundred thousand years.

As life forms had some fire essence in them, as we are warm blooded, sai came to mean alive, whence si could mean a life form. In Malay the Siamang ape or Gibbon, with arms as long as its legs, swings from branch to branch effortlessly. A tame one in Kuala Lumpur would circumnavigate the room going round the walls on the picture rails in seconds in swoops. The sibilant and the hum, the m consonant, were the only two consonants which could be pronounced continuously. All the others are just stops. So they were a pair, and whereas the flame was active and the sibilant was an outgoing of breath and active, while a hum was (almost) without breath and passive, so the sibilant was up like the flame and so the hum was down, and ma was heaviness (gravity) and lifelessness, death, the ground under our feet, the earth, and so earthing or planting seeds, and so planting human seed as well, and in Latin amare to love, from as [when] you were marai, planting your seed. So the meaning of live and active was in fire and derived from it; and what is more the flame had the instinct to go upwards whereas other dead things go down if not held up. So ash is burnt matter, that-flamed, but it is also an ash tree because ash trees are uppers, they have quick growing trunks with relatively few narrow branches, pushing their way through the jungle canopy to get to the upper fire, the sun and its light; whereas an oak, a-u-kai, was 'that-most-hard' wood. It spread out.

An upright stroke, a cut or a mark was used for counting, by marking them side by side, so sa or sai or si was an upright stroke and also meant one. The Romans used four uprights before finding the numbers getting too fat so diverted to a V for five and an X for ten, but a V and four uprights were too fat again so they had IX for nine and IV for four, taking one off instead of adding one on. The Arabs did it all much better with 9 different numerals each taking a single space to fill one column each, with a base of ten. You can see with just these few examples the meanings of the sibilant were sprouting out all over the place. Slowly but inexorably we were putting the world together in our heads, by a limitless expansion of meanings and the words to carry the meanings, all by way of metaphor. We still are. Our units from which we have composed the world are our ideas about it and the ways we fit them together by thinking ideologically. This ideological thinking is not really any real part of the world at all. The world doesn't think. It doesn't need to. It just does.

Of course you may say our heads are part of the world and our ideas are in turn in them, so they are part of the natural world. But this is not actually the case. Our heads, like the rest of us, are biological phenomena, part of the furniture of the universe. But our thinking is an activity, (we assume of our brains), and it is no more a part of our brains than the mileage of a car is part of the car. And what is more both our brains and the car are not really as we see them. After all, we all know these days a table top we're able to use as a flat surface supported at a convenient height actually comprises a collection of atoms locked into orbits under chemical and physical rules we have devised, and these atoms and rules in turn can be analysed in terms of a number of sub-atomic particles all slotted into the prior reality, and we finish up with Quarks and Black Holes and even former Black Holes which apparently lie behind the current Black Holes, and then we discriminate flavours and is it even different scents, or just about any description for items we think are there. So now what or where is the reality? I still take my meals off a table top, whilst all this underwork is churning below, and we have been developing more and more layers, each dependent and consonant in some way with the one before.

Linguistics pre-empts the philosophical issues; and none of the ideas are real, they are ideas, which are not real, they are fancies however clever they are. Now is the time to introduce the linguistic Wall Paper Theory too, simply because it buttons quite a lot of this theorising together, so you don't have to keep on chasing through the different levels of science, or is it the different sciences at different levels.

Now for the wallpaper, the theory. Every bit of the knowledge we have acquired has been acquired empirically. If you want to add any inspirational information, like for instance Adam in the garden or The Prophet Mohammad and the Angel Gabriel, who introduced it when Mohammad was unconscious with Malaria and had taken refuge at the back of a cave to try and get his temperature down, you have to add more senses for this information to have been received. But I haven't added them simply because I haven't received them.

All our information, from table tops, and legs to give them height and so we don't trip over them, has come from our senses: seeing hearing, smelling, tasting, and any other senses I have not spotted, but these are a very representative sample. To which you might say "Haven't we done well"; and I do. But I also say it is by now clear this is only a sensual wallpaper on which we have had to record everything we have learnt, and because of its relatively minimal sources of information it is perfectly clear it likely shares little with the actual reality which is effectively the actual wall which is what lies behind our sensual wallpaper, and this we can never sense or know because, by definition, it lies beyond our senses altogether. So the Wallpaper Theory shows that all our thinking is in terms of a wallpaper covering the actual reality; and where we have had to make out, (make up), our science(s). We are beginning to see, are we not, our ideological thinking gives us a rather inflated impression of our ability to pick out the reality; and a misplaced enthusiasm to go with it. Our judgment is, to put it bluntly, quite fraudulent. A statue has injected into it the whimsies the observer fancies, and the whimsies are invalid. The observer is the Punch in an ideological Punch and Judy Show: Physic, Physic, Physic! Universities are now adopting these techniques. Intellectual qualifications have all along involved ideological thinking, it comes in with science, and the thinking can be carried to extremes. Californian universities have professors convinced the Antifa ideology is worthy of credit. From this side of the pond, the old fashioned side, this is a degree of unreality which is staggering. It is Hitler's thinking precisely, dressed up as its opposite. There are supposed university professors quite unaware of the absurdity, as well as the mischief of their thinking. The States are one of the homes of slavery, and now in denial. Saudi is the other, and still at it, after thousands of years.

There is more. Our mathematics appear to justify our science. Old Albert Einstein – well he was young once – thought his mathematics proved his theories of the mix of space and time. But our mathematics is not any actual part of the furniture of the universe either, so that we can't use it as a priori to justify scientific theory. It is part of our own calculations we have been obliged to think out on the wallpaper. Where else? Of course the wallpaper in turn is merely the effective wallpaper, the ideas actually belong in our own minds. So is space/time just part of the furniture of our drawings on the wallpaper? Also our minds are not things; a mind is an abstract collective term for all of anybody's thinking. Our brains are physical phenomena. But our thinking is an activity, we suppose of our brains. Our ideological thinking has papered over the shortcomings of our ideas of reality, which are all at some remove from the wall behind the wallpaper.

When it comes to the ideological thinking of religions I must take care, because some religions do good, and opinions will differ as to which these are. The objection which has plagued ideological thinking is its persistence, exaggeration and refusal to allow criticism.

Perhaps in the case of religious beliefs the defence might be such postures are warranted. I do not think as much can be allowed to science. How many different sciences have there been in the last four hundred thousand years? Genesis is no longer science. Science changes with the generations. With minuscule slow changes it has gradually become a better guide which has recently much improved, to the extent that it has taken us to the moon, and back. That hardly guarantees all the other stuff, the old black holes apparently now supposed to be lurking behind the present ones, and all. Can we be sure we have the Big Bang right? Could there have been a string of them, in and out, in and out? And does it matter?

I am not letting all religions off. To start with, I describe the prehistoric religion of the Black Goddess Khali. The black refers to the dark of the night, nothing to do with skin colour, though of course in ideologies developed by those of minority skin colours today they may well claim ownership: and find the prehistoric goddess borrowing their colour offensive. Nevertheless the goddess Khali simply means black in Sanskrit, Aramaic and Hindustani. Her religion goes back many thousand years, it is not known how many. I think it is fair to say she was adopted first of all as an Arabic goddess. When the Divine Sphere was first probed by the human mind, it is believed the first divinities were all goddesses, mother gods. Aramaic was the only language the Prophet Jesus and the Prophet Mohammad spoke. Arabic, developed from Aramaic, was not in use until over a hundred years after the death of the Prophet Mohammad. Khali was believed by the Qureishi tribe in Mecca many thousands of years ago, nobody knows how many, and probably never will, but anyway thousands of years before The Prophet was born.

When a meteor slammed into Aden in the Yemen, or Underside [south] of Arabia, gouging out the crater in which the city of Aden is built, (it gives it some protection from the sun), a mass of meteorites from the tail of the meteor was spattered across Arabia and the Reed Sea. One, a black flint, landed beside the Qureishi Arab tribe's home village in the desert, and finding the splash mark in the sand where it struck, the Qureishi dug it out. It was between the size of a golf ball and a tennis ball, although they had the benefit of neither of these measures at the time. It had landed in a perfectly friendly manner without hurting anybody, and as it was black they guessed it was a Messenger sent by the Black Goddess to let them know She would be their Goddess and prosper them. They named their town Mecca in her honour, from the ancient Aramaic Mai-ka, Of the fall-the place; and they enclosed the splash as a holy site and called it Ka-a-ba, Place-that-[it]-went, and in due course the meteorite was mounted in the wall of the enclosure so the citizens could worship it there.

But Khali's influence soon led to a deterioration of the Qureishi's morality. As a Black Goddess She was a Goddess of the Night, of all the things of the dark, of death, destruction and deception, and required her followers to punish all unbelievers in Her, by killing them, so in time there would be no unbelievers left; and for this purpose She promised any of her followers who killed fifteen unbelievers seven virgins in the hereafter. It was at the time when the seven day week had just been established here on earth, (but we don't know when that was either) so it was a virgin for each day of the week, and then round and round again for eternity.

This apparently proved a sufficient incentive for doing the Goddess's bidding, and the Qureishi were soon taking so grievous a mulct from their neighbouring tribes they became known as "Wahabi" which in ancient Aramaic is terrorists, Wa-,shivering/fear/terror; -ha, rejoicing; -bai, in being/lifelong: a lifelong terrorist. The Qureishi, from Mecca, have forgotten what it means but as a long-held title are proud of it to this day. No ideologist has ever changed his mind, there is no room for that in ideological thinking. But Osama bin Laden was promising his jihadis, sworn to kill unbelievers in Islam, the religion of mercy, Khali's virgins in the hereafter. This is evidence he was a heretic, because when, way back, Khali promised her terrorists virgins in the hereafter, the next world was believed to be much the same as this one, with just the nasty bits left out, so it was not unreasonable to imagine you would arrive in the next world with your wedding tackle intact; but of course the Prophet Mohammad, like the Prophet Jesus and all the prophets of the Book, knew that the next world is a spiritual world and there is no sex, which is a physical matter. So Osama was an ignorant simpleton at best and fully deserved his violent death as a mass murderer to go with it. He was an ideologist, he had put together his own private religious ideology and could not change it. All the "Islamic" jihadis are heretical ideologists who flout the Koran. It was the Black Goddess Khali who required her followers to slaughter unbelievers, and Mohammad never did. His own two Jihads were both against his own Qureishi tribe who had been trying to kill him for forty years. It was an uncivilised time, well over a thousand years ago. It was the uncivilised idolatry of the Black Goddess, killing the other Arabian tribes, which was the background to the mission of The Prophet Mohammad and the establishment of Islam. I believe too it was the Qureishi tribe who found the inspiration to adopt Khali's violent religion. Belief is not automatic, you adopt it. If it were automatic there could hardly be any virtue in it, could there?

The Prophet managed to seize Mecca with a silent approach and a bloodless night time occupation of the city. The Qureishi awoke to find their city in the hands of Mohammad's Islamic army. He would have been entitled under the rules of war in those days to have massacred all his relatives. But instead he offered them all freedom provided they gave up Khali and became honest Muslims, which they all agreed to do. But some, evidently relying upon Khali's religious justification of deception decided to lie, and after the Prophet's death they were brazen enough to declare the Khaliphate as a committee of "Followers", but it actually is from the Aramaic Khali-phai, Khali-worshiping or Khali-worshipers. It was this gang, claiming to be Muslims, but actually Khali-worshipers, which killed all Ancient Egyptian speakers, who refused to abandon Ancient Egyptian, destroyed the Ancient Egyptian civilisation and fought their way all along the North African coast, killing the residents, and into Spain. Khali had never had such success until she was able to fight under the Islamic flag; every Khali worshiper had no problem securing his seven virgins for eternity in the hereafter (although they were of course imaginary); and the continued jihadi elements today, with Khali's virgins in the hereafter promised by Osama bin Laden make it absolutely clear he can not be a Muslim but must have been a heretic, with Khali's religion all along, whatever he himself thought. Similarly all the jihadi groups such as ISIS are loyal to the Black Goddess, whatever they may preach. It is a straight-forward demonstration of the power of ideology to maintain the belief of the ideologists, in the face of all the evidence. See Item 4 above which defines ideology. Ideological thinking is inward looking only and can only be right and can never change. Ultimately it is most often eventually best described as mad as the falsity burgeons.

Khali was established when the Adeni meteor fell. That may well have been even 10,000 years ago. Calcutta is from Khali-Cauta, Khali's Fort or Castle, (in this case a defended city, the black goddess at war with unbelievers all around her, and her virgins in the hereafter keeping her believers at war) so Khali worship spread from the west coast of Arabia to the eastern end of India, and now her religion is the heresy within Islam, so her religion may have covered a period five times as long as Christianity and twice as long as Judaism. In its original form it is not a religion which anyone with modern social beliefs could support. We must suppose the Sikhs have a revised version. They are only allowed to remove their underpants in the strictest privacy. Santok Singh, a civil liaison officer when I was in the Malayan jungle, (he spoke Cantonese to interrogate any captured terrorists), he could not cool off in the river after a day patrolling with the rest of us, as he was unable to remove his underpants and would have had to wear them wet after bathing in them, and anyway he could not really even be seen with only his underpants on. I never caught him with his trousers off. I sometimes wondered if the underpants were religiously plain or religiously coloured. I made it a rule never to question anyone about their religion. It can only lead to misunderstanding I don't think the Qureishi, Khali's original worshipers, were required to even wear underpants, indeed I don't think the first pair of pants had been stitched at that time. Clothing was of the night shirt variety so as not to take too much stitching. So he sat on the bank, along with the naked Senoi aborigine boys - who had gathered on the bank for the porn show. The aborigine women had fled into the jungle. The aboriginal menfolk men were not well endowed, and were fully clothed with a small bag of woven bamboo and a bamboo cord round their waists and between their legs. Just like Santok, they could not take their "chawat" off except in the strictest privacy, (under their blanket in their long house).

CHAPTER 5

IDEOLOGIES IN THE STONE AGE
WHEN WE FIRST LEARNT TO SPEAK

Well, there is more I have already written which is relevant to ideology in the Stone Age, but I am separating it altogether from Marx. The nearest you can get to the Marxist gallimaufry on the dialectic is Stone Age sex theory (boy + girl = progeny), which appears to have been introduced initially in the Lithic scheme of primitive vowelisation. Our first sallies into reasoning came out reeking of the subconscious soup from which they sprang, and it was quite strong stuff. See below. Clear thinking in precise terms rules it out, but daydreaming fishing for original thinking can still conjure it up.

I am obliged to S R Fischer (A History of Language, Page 103) for his notice of Rongo Rongo, the prehistoric writing of Easter Island. Some 25 mantras in this script survive, from an unknown time ago, and we don't know who by, most of them appearing superficially to be sketchy mnemonics of various bizarre sexual copulations. But I think they are records of dialectical thinking recorded as fundamental meditation by the Easter Islanders of the day, whoever they were. Needless to say I see them as childish and wrongheaded also, but not however as evidence of the pornographic mentality of savages that the literal reading of all the copulating would otherwise suggest. Their dialectics were just as dialectical as anything Hegel or Marx turned out, if clothed in language derived from idioms Mrs Grundy would hardly have cared for. Moreover there is added to Hegel the further insight whence originally sprang the dialectic, arising like a miasma from the dream world of the subconscious, borne on the confusion of sexual excitement with the purely intellectual stimulus of the Eureka feeling. The Dialectic owes something to a misprision of a plainly sexual pattern. Nikita Khrushchev may have been getting more out of banging his shoe on the table than his fellow United Nations delegates were aware of. Perhaps at bedrock orgasm is the plain man's Eureka. The latter is said to have sent Archimedes straight from his bath romping through the streets with no clothes on at all. It undoubtedly was for him a great excitement. He had discovered specific gravity, no doubt worked up into an ideology.

But to return to the basics of Rongo Rongo as devised by the Easter Islanders, way back, whenever it was when they were around: the inscriptions (all wood carvings) appear to comprise simple telegram style statements in the form $A + B = C$, glossed as A copulates with B producing C. Whether even math itself arises from the sexual metaphor thrown up by the subconscious is here a red herring, but it could be so. Fischer cites the following example: (Te) Manu mau [phallus = ki 'ai' ki rota ki] ika [ka pute] ra'a". This is translated as "All the birds copulated with the fish: there issued forth the sun". He extracts the elements actually glyphed: Man'u (all the birds) mau (all impregnated) ika (the fish), ra'a (Ra'issued forth). But to look further at what the Easter Islanders were actually thinking we may note that bird is Manu, two phonemes ma-and-nu which can carry the very early semantic contents mass and none, and the final -u can provide the alternative meaning, at the same time too, of 'all'. A bird for the Easter Islanders was defined as Brer Weightless. Compare the Australian aboriginal Ba-Ji for bird, which meant Go-Up, those life forms able to overcome their weight, which causes the rest of us to fall to the ground if unsupported. Bird in English is similarly from Bai-rai-dai, Going-raised-does. They too are identified as go-ups. In Malaya there is similarly the Siamang Ape, an acrobatic long armed Gibbon, Si-a-ma-ang, Brer-un-weight-one, Brer Weightless. Mau as well as the earth and so the massive element and so the mass or weight of anything might also be used for earth, earthing and so the planting of seed, and so impregnation, or even the gestation in the ground or in the womb. In Egypt the god Amun, The Ever Loving One, carried the same semantic content as the Latin amare to love, a-ma-are, as[when]-impregnating-verb ending marker. In Malay mau means simply to like or want; but in aboriginal Senoi it covers lust and sexual possession as well. Words start out with a wide coverage when in short supply and assume more specific meanings as they multiply. Ika for fish on Easter Island is the same as ikan in Malay and ika in numerous New Guinea tongues, and the Malay ikan on numerous other islands in the Pacific. I-ka-'n is Single-body-one, Brer-limbless. It was the "ma-na" or mental presentation or conceptions of these species, not just their physical conception, which came together in the Easter Islanders' minds when they became conjoined. Copulation was merely their robust and vivid paradigm for any linking together. It was a conjunction. How better to anchor the idea in Sunny Jim's adolescent mind?

So it was simply the elements of weightlessness of the birds and simplicity of structure of the fish, its reduction to basic outline shape, with no limbs, which came together and coming together reached their apogees in the character of the sun; quintessentially weightless and flighty, a super bird, and at the same time the ultimate in minimalist configuration, not even a single fin to keep it aloft. Thus it was meditation for Rongo Rongo boys and girls: spot the combinatory characters! It is bogus science of course but you can see it is science of a sort. (How many sciences have we believed in our first four hundred thousand years of ideological thinking?) It is also demonstrably dialectical. A fish is not the antithesis of a bird at first sight, but on reflection the water surface, a major natural interface (d'), divides them just as a distinction (d') divides the categories x and not x: the fish at home swimming below the interface and the bird above it, and both by fin-beat. If the bird is thetic, the fish is antithetic, or else the other way around. One is the reflection of the other with the natural boundary (d') between them. The sun in turn mimics the flying fish, up out of the water with a fine swoop at dawn into the empyrean with the birds, and then disappears down into the deep at dusk back into the fishy element again. These are certainly simple metaphors, but they are not mad or bad. Some fish had an Apollonian temper and would fly short distances while some birds exhibited a remarkable aquarian propensity, diving to join the fish. This put them in the latter category as well, with a little bit of what they fancied on either side of the boundary. The abstraction of the abstract adjectivals, the weightless and the simple-shaped adjectival elements, are both characters of our own reductive science, a potent dialectic indeed now with better terms to it, distinguishing (itemising) and then recognising their common elements and bringing them together, nowadays as in chemical formula rather than as man and wife. It is the genesis of the method which is of principal interest when contemplating the origins of thinking. The bird has grown legs for landing gear but the fish remains completely fishy dying when it lands out of water.

"Pisces" for fish, from the phonemes "pai-sa-kai-sa", which can be analysed semantically with the following meanings, pai, of-the limbs, sa, action, kai, of the body, sa, action: he uses the leg-action-of his body, Brer Motile Body. It is metaphor all along, and so only makes sense in the terms in which it was originally conceived. The fish is born in water and dies out of it but the sun is born out of the water and dies into it, so the sun gets that from the bird, since the bird drowns in water; but how is a bird born from it? That is the conundrum for meditation. Is an egg sufficiently watery to keep the metaphorical cat's cradle going? The kingfisher was thought to be born from water, at sea, perhaps he was given this role because he clearly had a natural affinity for water and spent so much time diving back into it. We can see the dialectic is silly but the Easter Islanders couldn't. We may be smarter, and the Easter Islanders were certainly simple, but not all that much when you look at the twentieth century, our culture ragged out by Hegel and Marx, and the dialectic still a plank in the intellectual firmament even now, after so many millions dead from the hedonistic massage of the psyche by this methodology, apparently still teasing professors in Californian universities, some of whom apparently even support Antifa, the Marxist based dialectic which surely puts them on about the same level as the Easter Islanders with the birds and fishes copulating together to form the sun.

Perhaps the Jewish God was the first, even the only dialectical God. Jehovah, the Jewish God, that Christians witness (with Pagan overtones), was originally "Yahweh" or, in original phonemes, "Ia-u-Ai", the magic combination of original vowelisation, a, i and u, pronounce aaa, iii and ooo. So in Jaweh were originally the vowels 2-1-3-1-2, I-A-U-A-I, which orthodox Jews at one time preferred not to reveal, but held them covered by referring to God as Adonai instead, because their secret virtue they believed was in the vowelisation, IA-U-AI. There is a symmetry about the central Lithic completive dual vowel u, pronounced oo in English but in Semitic languages often articulated as a semi consonant Wa. "He-extension-both-extension-He" appears to be the semantics concealed in the original appellation. "The Universal and Eternal": a dialectical God with omnipotent aspects spatial and temporal brought together in Final Synthesis: The Single Extensive, Both, One Eternal. We are counting one, two, both of them, from a time before iteration had been fully worked out, I guess possibly at the beginning of speech, when we all thought in these phonemes, not yet combined into words. It may be bad math but it is basic for religion, a dialectical trinity, perhaps even prefiguring Einstein's Space-Time-Both of them: anyway a thinking man's god, unlike the Christian Trinity which is a comforter for everybody, and not an intellectual secret for the intellectually adept like Jaweh. All this is not all that far on from the origins of speaking hundreds of thousands of years ago. But in all this time Sapiens and then Sapiens Sapiens has not changed his spots; and only the Lithic Hypotheses make sense of any of this surprising persistence over so long a time, or indeed has any knowledge whatever of the origins of speaking. Is it just speech which distinguishes Homo Sapiens from Homo Sapiens Sapiens; both still the same species Homo Erectus underneath?

Hard science (physics) treats its categories as real. An atom is supposed to be really out there, bolstered by the perfectly valid theory that the world is what it is and not another thing. The same rule is applied to subatomic particles and their qualities. But it actually must be all a ghastly mistake. Sure, there are definite things out there; but we know they are not the same as we perceive them to be. Of course Emanuel Kant already knew this, but he did not know what they were. In science this is a truism; a solid table such as Doctor Johnson kicked, or any other solid body, is in fact a congeries of dancing particles with electromagnetic fields, and most of the space is just that – space between the particles – when scientifically described. Our fingers, similarly composed, simply bounce off the table's fields when they encounter the table's "surface". Moreover red is not really red; it is a frequency band of electromagnetic radiation, to which our optical sensors respond with the mental experience we know as red. What we experience as red is by no means the same as the electronics which trigger the experience. We may be the recipient of rays, but what and where is the screen on which these phantoms are displayed. We do not now imagine there is a manikin behind the eye reading the pictures from behind as we can sometimes catch sight of them on the iris from in front. When we sit on a pin and it punctures the skin we dislike what we fancy we feel. But it is not the same thing as the physical reactions of the nerves involved. The problem is the scientific terms we use to redefine what we regard as real are also figments as we present them to ourselves. Science provides us with linguistic refinements for the most part. That is not an excuse for walking away and going over to mystic illuminations, but it is certainly an opportunity.

Molecular biology copies the hard sciences. But it does not treat of thinking, only of the brain, and the neurons in it. We are left with an apparently unbridgeable divide between the mind (the thinking) and the brain. The mind is simply an abstract term for all your thinking. It is not a physical entity and can not be located anywhere, in the brain or anywhere else. Science is reasonably content with this, provided the things which have been scientifically detected out there are given precedence: molecular biology is prior to psychoanalytic theory for instance. Examining the brain is scientific. Psychoanalysis (which claims to deal with mental events) is a "cultural construct".

Unfortunately, the distinction between science and cultural constructs is not as helpful as it at first appears, since science too is actually a cultural construct as well. It is a myth the scientist directly accesses the real world and his determinations are therefore objective. The history of the discipline immediately rubbishes any such idea. This realisation must come as an unwelcome shock to anyone who has walked on the moon – or even sent the walker there. He or she is rightly persuaded the science is objective (gets veridical results) in a way Freud's and other fantasists' waffle is not and does not. Moreover he scores highly for abstraction and precision. Freud too is lavish with his abstractions but he scores less highly for precision. Clearly some cultural constructs are better than others; and what makes them better has to do with the rigour with which fickle fancy is controlled and subjected to severe testing by comparing it with independently deduced "facts" and circumstances. It is the match which validates the science, not the method. Scientists alas are as human as the rest of us, or more so, and often remain unaware of this.

Our consciousness can be (and I think actually should be) analysed in a continuum of developing crispness and informativeness of semantic content. I have labelled the stages in this continuum with Greek letters – chiefly to raise the tone of the piece as mathematicians often do; although the Greek letters do have lip smacking qualities germane to my purpose too.

(1). Psi (Ψ), perhaps symbolising a boundary crossing (or perhaps a cactus), designates those sensations which reach our brains and trigger immediate mental events: Ouch!, Hark!, Hot!, Ha!, Wa!, Hard!, Sour!, etc. You hardly need any intelligence for the job. If you are awake and reasonably sober you should get the message. A Chimp would. But I go on from Hot! etc to include in this same sector the other more specific raw emotional and adjectival responses to stimuli: Horror!, Horny!, High!, Hiss!, Hate, Hurtful, Hearty, Hellish, etc. An initial h is not a requirement but it is often a guide because the original element "Ha!" is the sudden compulsive explosion of breath due to shock or exhilaration. The prototype is the Pleistocene foolish boy (or girl) picking up a white hot stone in mistake for charred wood, to throw it back into the burning hearth, compulsively exclaiming "Ha!" for hot as the finger roasts. The list can be extended to individual taste, and often has been; sometimes with bizarre results when early psychologists have been compiling lists of instincts. There is virtually no limit for a sophisticated mind to the categorisation of primitive traumatic promptings capable of being identified and labelled. But it is probable our first speakers contented themselves with very few; so we shall not bother with all those expansions which are possible. Psi just stands for the crude rude initial primitive psychic output, as input for anything to follow.

(2). Next to Psi is Phi (Φ), originally an Egyptian rude gesture carried over into Greek script (the erect pai originally penetrating the circle rather than merely crossing it), but here employed for the whole adjacent area of mentality, the identification of phenomena, including the Phi (Φ) which appears to have started out as Tarzan's penis, here superimposed upon his partner's pudenda, originally penetrating it, originally pronounced as pai-hei, a diminutive piece of Bai-hei, flesh-orgasmic. Anyway, this is the phenomenal level of thinking, simply taking in and mentally digesting crude input, identifying "things" presented to the senses; along with commonsensical ideas of causation, etc: pre-analytical thinking, just in learning terms coming to grips with vocabulary. Phi is adequate for some simple abstractions and analogies arising from them. Given the initial crudity of Psi (Ψ), identification of things is already by comparison an abstract process. Phi recognises both form and function, rescuing us from prior all-adjectival guesswork. This is conscious thinking at last, such as we know as commonplace today. A chimp by contrast is mostly stuck in Psi, with only the tip of his accomplishment nosing into Phi, unless dragged forward by human intervention. But the mere identification of phenomena wins no prizes for thinking.

(3). Eventually – after many millennia – we got scientific. I have called reasoned marshalling of phenomena in the mind Pi (Π). It is crisper than Phi and conspicuously requires reasoning. Pi is a skin or surface, nothing to do with the penis. It still allows for a great deal of erroneous ratiocination, but it is where we are at today. Pi is for Pattern, a layout on a surface, conspicuous scheming, everything from the realisation there are regularities in human experience to the modernists' fancied theory of everything. It takes in magic and religion as well as science. It is a broad bailiwick. But it only takes one thin mental slice at a time out of the rich complexity of the reality it seeks to capture, and it is only a remote representation at one remove from it. Most of humanity's mistakes naturally enough are in this latest sector of intellectual activity, crammed up against the current end of it – including the idea there could or should be a theory of everything.

(4). This leaves Ro (P) for the Reality, confronting the Psi, Phi, Pi series but in no way part of it. Our intellect doodles on the wallpaper while Ro is the real underlying wall our doodling is supposed to represent; which is contrary to the naïve and popular idea that our doodling is progressively getting closer to the real wall and may hope to alight on it, with an ultimate all-inclusive theory, given sufficient time and attention. That is a category error. It confuses the wall with the wallpaper. Our ideas must always remain at one remove from reality for as long as we recognise a world outside ourselves, since the wallpaper on which we draw turns out (in reality!) to be papered on the insides of our own heads, a mental construct, compiled from our sensual responses, which of course are by nature essentially subjective. Our linguistic and even our mathematical presentations remain just metaphors, in an intellectual medium human enough, but always unreal. There is no Holy Grail in science, there is only representation, more or less remote.

I like this scheme of things because it points up the absurdity of Napoleonic thinking and the other methodologies of the asylum which seek to illuminate Pi by recourse to Psi, as if inspiration were superior to reason, an escape from hard thinking by going back to the primitive end of the spectrum expecting to tunnel from Psi all the way round to come up again at the other end out in front of Pi. That is an illicit move in my gaming. So there you have it. Psi, Phi and Pi is all we know on earth, and in that order; and perhaps even all we need to know – since the rest is developed from the study of Lithic thinking, all unapologetically in the third category, Pi, yet not without benefit of Psi and Phi also.

There is a recent mental module theory which proposes the human mind was divided into separately functioning departments until recently. It is quite unproven. But there is indeed a problem in the archaeological record. How is it that we were fly enough to flake away at hand axes with such increasing precision and yet, for half a million years or so, too thick to get around to decent thinking? The cognitive neurologists have come up with the idea our brains were divided into modules not consciously connected, so that while we could learn the tricks of the trade within any module, we could not apply what now seem to us the lessons of what we had learned to do, outside the module concerned. What modules there might have been is then up for grabs: suggested are sexual (for reproductive skills), social (for clan collaboration), technical (for flaking flints etc), natural (for catching game to eat), and eventually linguistic (for communicating between modules as well as with the neighbours). So when we learned to speak we broke the partitions between the modules. That may have been why the modules were proposed so language could remove them. It fits in quite well with the idea language has been our biggest clever bit ever, making all the difference so we are now Sapiens Sapiens instead of just single Sapiens, (and the same old Erectus underneath). The Homo is nothing to do with humus, we are not Earthlings. I have derived it from Ha-u, both enjoying, ma-u, the orgasm. With animals, apart from the Bonobo miniature Chimpanzee, (whose enthusiasm for sex has made it impossible to display in public), sex tends to be nasty brutish and short.

Seventy years ago when I was at Oxford as an undergraduate, after five years war service, the students who were studying PPP, the latest syllabus taking in Philosophy, Politics and also Psychology in place of the Economics of PPE, used the old British psychologist MacDougall as exemplar of this temptation to fabricate psychic modules (he just called them instincts in his case) in excessive profusion, and we coined the coffee drinkers' term "a silly MacDougall". There may still be something of this "silly MacDougall" abroad in the Halls of Academe even today.

The inter-modular incapacity really makes better sense if you adopt the position that over this half million years or so the hominid brain simply was not thinking consciously at all (or anyway very little) as we understand it, more just apprehending individual skills subconsciously by looking and doing, the old apprentices' way; so that the marvel is better rephrased: how was it that this brainless wonder was making tools without thinking about it at all, simply by following subconscious promptings to copy, without really knowing what he was doing, as we understand it today, at all? It goes against the grain of common sense at first; but then parrots can copy human speech, with a noticeably limited range also, and nobody thinks they think through what they are saying or have any knowledge of exactly how they do it. They follow their instinct to squawk the squawks they hear. In the same way perhaps our forebears followed their instincts to copy the flaking they saw, fine tuning the artefact as the parrot fine tunes its articulation. If you think about it, we can ourselves still do as much, for instance when we sing when we compose the notes and tunes without any need to direct our vocal organs to do it. Perhaps hand axes were effectively sung. Certainly, without words to work with, hominids could not lay layer upon layer of thinking as we can today. They were in exactly the same pickle as trying to do algebra without any notation. It is not theoretically impossible but it is extremely difficult; and without the ability to have a solid (unified categorical) idea and hold it in the mind so as to be able to come back to it with the degree of precision required for further thinking about it, it is indeed impossible.

The question we should be asking ourselves when it comes to getting inside a dumb hominid's mind is what ideas was he having? It is a question which has not been asked because it appears to be unanswerable. We have probably compounded the difficulty by seeking to preserve speaking for a late achievement of Sapiens Sapiens, when in reality our primitive hominid forebears were already articulate yet still pretty beastly with it. Moreover I think you could initially go bashing flints just for the fun of it like a gorilla drumming on his chest, to see and hear them break: "Just look what I can do!"; and then you cut yourself on a sharp edge which results from your flaking. You don't have to go looking for tools. You simply trip over them;

they find you. All you need to be able to remember is what hurt last time; and then, and this is what made you human, you have to go back for more of the same, just like the squirrel does after burying his nuts. If his tail were not so bushy he would be half human at least: he is relatively feeble but quick on the draw and bites. He even has hands, and all that has held him back is the refractoriness of stone – he can't break it. We are not so much featherless bipeds as giant squirrels who shed our pretty tails; and we had the wit or just the good fortune to grow big enough to break stones. You just need hands and a bit of beef behind them for the trick; and memory first of course, but that came in with the herbivores, knowing which bits to bite.

That is a kind of thinking, but it would not win many prizes. It is thinking about thinking which is what we really mean when we think about thought; and consciousness is a completely different thing. Every living thing is conscious in the limited sense it is responsive to inputs. A fly contemplates the fly swat and is only defeated when we perforate the weapon so the pressure wave is subtly altered to deceive him, and all this without a single thought in his head that we would recognise as such. None of this fits in too well with the present ideas of the cognitive neurologist, wrapped up in his study of the microphysics of the brain on the grounds you can't ignore science, or even with the cognitive archaeologist looking for inspiration in his catalogue of stone tools. With minds trained to think in terms of their bits and bobs, they invent the hominid mind in their image, adding blinkers to taste to account for the hominid's deficiencies. That methodology is flawed. They believe our forebears were dumb, but they allow them the mental paraphernalia of craftsmen today, only cutting off the bits which elude them in the record.

It is better to start with nothing and think of stone tools as coprolites from the mental digestive system. Nobody nowadays thinks of his stomach as an organ of rational activity but the job it does puts tool making in the shade. I am not forgetting that nowadays we have minds capable of thinking of a complexity almost to match the stomach. But looking around it is clear it is still something of a novelty. Moreover you can easily have a brain without using it, or at least without using it for thinking very much. It wasn't even put there for thinking; it was put there for running the enterprise, as the control centre, a job it continues to do well enough even when we are not thinking but dead drunk or in a coma. The thinking is an accidental and inessential spin off from the nervous system developed for another purpose, namely running the phenotype's engine room. This is in fact the classic evolutionary pattern of adapt and make do, which has engineered novelties galore (conspicuously eyes which focus for instance) as spin-offs from other previous facilities. Although we may value thinking highly, it is not all that important in Darwinian terms. Indeed it is usually regarded – correctly in fact – as outside the rest of evolution. With speech and education, it is argued, survival of the fittest takes a new turn and selection ceases to be natural and becomes cultural instead. Or at least cultural selection is added to the pile. After all we spend a good deal of time these days spoking nature's wheel with medicines and therapies of one kind and another, and even borrowing and diverting her techniques for our own purposes, monkeying with genes.

We can see now that with a bit more flexibility the bishops might well have won in 1859, and the churches might not now be facing annihilation from scientific progress. They should have dumped the body and argued for the mind as its successor in the struggle for survival, leaving aside where the mind comes from and discussing how we should handle it now we have it as it is. It would be uncharitable to suggest the cognitive gentry are still in something of the same bind as the bishops, but certainly their attempt to treat conscious thinking simply under the biological rubrics of the day – to keep it all scientific – is quite simply misplaced. It is misplaced because with thinking you can produce it cheap and pile it high - according to Chomsky infinitely high - something which does not occur in nature. The mind, and mental activity in Pi (Π), is sui generis. So we can get better results by letting the mind go free, and then of course in tranquillity mulling over what we have, with all the sagacity science can muster. It is a question of de Bono's hats. Academics working on the brain wear one big sombrero with a brim so big it drops to the ground, so that they never take it off (or see out from under it), because doffing it is too much of a discard, unless they are drunk or dreaming. We should not urge them to get drunk but certainly a bit of undisciplined dreaming, allowing their modules to go free and just listening to the music does help. It amounts to a new science of dumping. Einstein would have approved. He surely must have dumped his bits and bobs and launched his mind into empty space with awesome abandon. We know this in fact because he said so. At one time he wrote off language altogether. But he recollected it in tranquillity, as we all must if we wish to avoid the asylum.

To come back to our origins in hominid cognition, they evidently managed without much thinking. Why can we not allow that they simply did not do much conscious thinking at all? Or at least they did not think with the attention to it that we are accustomed to. They worked things out "by guess and by golly" with admirable perspicacity. I am arguing that with hominids it was mostly by golly, the surprise and delight of finding something which worked when you went through the motions; so that it was a spin off from the instinct to show off which underlay our intellectual development ab origine. For most of the last million years it simply did not occur to do much thinking out loud – the chimp in us got no lessons from futurity in those days. It was just a case of accepting what occurred.

This chapter so far has – I admit it – skirted and skated round the nub of its proper subject matter, how initially we were habituated to thinking and in what terms we thought. We have come across some pointers merely: the Psi, Phi, Pi, Ro sequential analysis of the mental spectrum; the adjectival mind; the source of categorisation in the recognition of the prior distinction (and so eventually nouns derived from adjectives); together with a good deal of poking fun at those persistent aficionados of the atavistic dialectic. This has been a deliberate preliminary in order to clear away some at least of the commonly held misapprehensions which would otherwise immediately confront what follows.

No doubt before speaking the mind dwelt on what was presented to it, just as it still does today. It is most probable we have extracted and distilled our intelligence from contemplation of the world around us, as well as within us; if only because it is difficult to see where else we might have got it from. There was, it may be presumed, a grave tendency to snatch at knowledge and jump to all the wrong conclusions, based on perfunctory resemblances (e.g. the fish, birds and sun in Rongo Rongo) mad metaphors and whimsical prepossessions (e.g. universal copulations) just as is the case today. Half a million years ago (say) when primitive speech was forming, or better when our utterances were being developed to carry an increasing semantic loading, the most difficult bit to accommodate (in our minds these days) about this early stage of prehistory is probably the degree of ignorance, and incapacity to cope, which generally obtained. Illiteracy we know, but inarticulacy is largely unexplained, and general inarticulacy is almost impossible to comprehend. With no speech we must have been nearer monkeys than men so far as our mentality was concerned, regardless of what studies of contemporary physique may reveal. How can we visualise this instinctive brute, with no conscious grasp of reality, beginning to assemble the mental tools for conscious ratiocination, confronting himself and his world? Small wonder there has been a desperate inclination to look to the monkey world for guidance. How does a chimp think? He is pre-articulate. But he is surprisingly teachable, given enough time and effort. What is largely lacking is Simian intention; they are lazy brutes, mentally sluggish, failing if left to themselves to make the most of themselves. Even today we can see the pattern is inter-specific, it is at work inter species. It is a fair bet our hominid forebears were in the same boat. Their grey matter was there but it lay largely untapped because they did not have the foresight or interest to start using its full potential, to start building its potential, hard work at the end of a day taken up with making their way. That is one reason why it is most likely it developed in the first place for some other purpose altogether. There can hardly have been any selective advantage in an enlarged organ which lay unused. Perhaps it provided balance for the upright stance, or finger control for all sorts of handy jobs, etc, all without making use of conscious thought. The chimp's own accomplishments solely concern its own betterment, e.g. signing "Gimme banana". There is no intention there to direct anything else.

Yet chimps are far from autistic. They know each other. They can relate to humans. So can a horse, a dog or a cat, of course. A cow or a sheep can accept us but hardly contribute anything intentional. Of course a cow can readily distinguish a daisy from a blade of grass. But she probably does not think about them. That is the point. A monkey and an inarticulate hominid are both in great part cow. But at the same time, the hominid, it turns out, is on a roller coaster to ratiocination – if we speed up the process a bit. This was certainly tied up with a substantial accumulation of grey matter inside his skull, the lid of which rose to accommodate it. Or else the grey matter simply expanded to fill the gap made by the rising lid? That in turn might easily have been from some uninspiring circumstance, like more chewing – or less (with cooked food perhaps). Meanwhile hominid instincts will have been purely animal, though his brain provided unprecedented and unlooked for opportunities for building and retaining thought patterns on a vastly extended scale.

I am inclined to think, since there appears as far as one can tell to have been a contemporaneity, that mental usage grew from the taming of fire, on top perhaps of an increased meat diet now that it could be cooked. It literally made us all sit up and think; our culture comes from naked seminars around the hearth, with our warm bellies full of cooked meat, and our warm minds most probably thinking of sex for desert. After all, not only cooked viands but also the warmth around the hearth gazing into the coals must have applied adaptive pressures upon the human frame including the brain. We talk of animals coming into heat. Our hominid forebears were animals every day coming into heat. I believe it was this unnatural heating which led to an enormous increase in the sexual athleticism of the human race. It is not hard to see, when one pictures to oneself any group of hominids, their minds still largely empty, their bellies full, hunkered for the pleasing and relaxing warmth close together around the hearth, perhaps in the mouth of their cave, all of them as bare as the day they were born. The warmth, as well as the proximity and availability of adjacent bodies, must have stimulated the adult parties present sexually. These early folk were inclined, in the absence of ratiocination, to do what came naturally; and what it was can surely fairly easily be rumbled. You do not need to be a medical practitioner to notice that with heat the vascular system expands increasing the heart rate so that inter alia more blood is pumped to the genitalia, and in turn there is an automatic and involuntary engorgement. Surely our bare bottomed forebears will have noticed this also, on a daily basis. Even a natural warm climate encourages sex, leaving Britons, originally the Peri-Taun-i, Periphery-of the world-ones, notoriously under privileged in that department. That is the real reason, in this air age, for the annual flight of citizens from countries in Northern climes to the sun. With the sun, young folk become ravers and older folk are miraculously enlivened. The Mediterranean littoral has always built a macho male. The steamier African continent is also renowned for its sexual prowess. In India the worship of sex is most highly developed, and armed with the Karma Sutra lives are probably shortest because of the overworked heart, added to an ill supplied stomach. Not only is there this connection between climate and sexual activity, surely much increased in a much hotter artificial microclimate around the hearth, but there is also, just as importantly, a change in the ambiance of the sexual relationship. Both sexes are relaxed as well as stimulated by the warmth of the occasion. Orgiastic sex releases more emotion. It could have been this bomb burst of emotion which triggered the birth of the thinking man. If so intellectual activity comes from emotionalism. Long after he was capable of any further orgasm, Tarzan found he still enjoyed thinking about it. He really got thinking. It was perhaps overwhelming sexual emotion which drove him to think, to trawl up out of his subconscious this reflection of what drove him, for further savouring in relative tranquillity. This was mankind hooked on thinking, faut de mieux, his mind in a pink haze as he focused on his earlier pleasuring and planned more for the future.

In short we have swum to civilisation through a positive sea of sexuality which was the original Open Sesame to fully conscious thinking; and the male genitals have burgeoned beyond all necessity compared with the other apes, simply from countless generations of obsessive and addictive over use, aeons of frenetic sexuality, and of course the necessary selection for it. It was around the hearth also, I imagine, that the ladies will have first got out their needles and tailored stomachers of animal skin for their menfolk to keep their bellies warm out hunting and lively on their return, with the innate animal liveliness of the furry animal life-support systems they were borrowing. Ratiocination is really just refined emotion and without it learning is dreary in the extreme. Thinking is a vehicle just like speaking is, and we have now perhaps identified the original burden of human thought. We pile Ossa on Pelion when we speak as well. Learning demands emotion today. Some teachers are charismatic, others are not. That largely determines the outcome.

Mrs Grundy has by now turned her face to the wall, but we should perhaps meanwhile turn our attention in turn to the Reverend Mr. Grundy, not yet comfortable with the idea of orgiastic copulation over aeons, courtesy of the divine flame, however ancient. Sexual fantasy was indeed the first full dress rehearsal for the real performance (thinking), and (at the risk of being accused of merely punning) this first full mental address – the word here used in its verbal sense – gave us our first fully realised mental addresses (nouns) sufficient for all subsequent mental rehearsals, images imprinted in the cortex as fully conscious images. Moreover the very same images are, I believe, still there, the lingam still firmly imprinted in the lingo, and only the concealment of the subconscious mind preserving a fragile decorum.

For the Revd G we can cite the Egyptian head god Amun (Lithic Aa-Mau'n) "Eternally both inseminator and gestator", "The Ever Loving, both sexes", crude forerunner indeed of the all encompassing love of the Christian Deity. It should perhaps be explained Ma comprised a number of derivative semantic contents, including particularly here that of earth and the earthing (planting) of seed and thus both insemination and germination; while Latin amare, to love, from the Egyptian via the Greek, (Lithic A-ma-are), 'As when planting', the male or mali role [mali is Hindi for gardener, ma-lai, earth-leveller], as in Malaya, the Garden of

Eden, or at least that peripheral hilly bit of it left above water when the melting of the Ice Age flooded Eden, the Eastern Garden Land, now 160 feet under the South China Sea. The resultant diaspora colonised both Sumer and then Babylon and then Egypt. It was Amun too who first pursued fully the drive for life after death in its most literal institutional form, again prefiguring Christian belief. This in turn may be why recent biblical scholarship has located Moses, and the Mosaic religion still professed by the Jews, in Egypt (The Fatherland in Egyptian) with Moses a priest of the Aton (the Eternal birth canal, the sun birthing light into the world each day in Egyptian) and even possibly a subsequent dissident Pharaoh (The Devine Penis in Egyptian). If this were the historical pattern the congeners of the Egyptian language to be found in Malay, otherwise hard to explain, would fall into place.

Recall, after all, is the missing element in subconscious thinking, the mind retains no imprint of this activity, the job is done without a record, certainly without a record in any detail. I believe that the taming of fire and the consumption of cooked protein meals around the convivial hearth led to sexual consummations, no hair pulling needed any more, and sweet dreams thereafter, still remembered on waking. Life became all Rongo Rongo, and this had important consequences quite additional to sexual activity. There was a spin off, as so often with physical evolution. What was sauce for the sexual gander was also sauce for the mother goose. The same breakthrough into conscious appreciation of hitherto subconscious responses, what was formerly the dream on autopilot, could now after the breakthrough lead to conscious appreciation, focused attention, and to quite other diverse matters; prideful consideration for instance of tapping out a hand axe, that is the lesser delights of getting it right at work, of mastering the initially refractory medium which too turned out to yield to slick technique. Wherever there was pleasure in such ego-massage the new found mind would wander. The Scrimshaw had begun, leaving Wayland Smith behind, doomed, with just the heavy work to do.

It is necessary to point out here, to enable Mrs Grundy to return to the debate, as well as to check any young blades seeking to recapture their authentic roots, that none of this has any current implications for human thinking or conduct, other than the reflection that honesty is often the best policy for understanding. To argue that nothing has changed in half a million years, or even just the thick end of it, is blatantly absurd. What has survived as an adaptive response on the part of the human physique as a result of this outburst of frenetic sexual activity long ago, with the fair sex in charge of stoking the fire all day, 24 x 7, is a degree of independence of the menstrual cycle, so that sex is available at all times, a happy circumstance we apparently share only with the Bonobo Pigmy Chimps – and they have evidently achieved it without the benefit of the hearth. We are the only two Hoka Hoka species on earth, the procreational function dumped in pursuit simply of raw stimulation, same sex as well as heterosex. It is a bizarre accident, no part of the original scheme of things (which was for genuine procreation), resulting from suddenly introduced long term overheating in the Pleistocene. Fascinated by the fire, the heat and the flame together, the mind has confronted and out-stared nature. It is the price we have paid for our culture. Now we are stuck with this outmoded fillip we hardly need any more. We are Homo Sapiens, first just Homo. It meant Ia-u-mau, It that-one-shape, and so the same, but it also was Haiu-maiu, Rejoicing both-the insemination both, Both enjoying Sex. With animals, sex is nasty brutish and short, the male may secure his partner with his teeth. I witnessed a mallard Drake inadvertently actually drowning his duck by climbing on top and holding her under water in his beak so she drowned.

I think the original sexual reverie is probably responsible, as much as the present promptings of the gonads, for the sexual content of so much of present day psychologising. Certainly, so far as language is concerned, the sexual prototypes of so much of the lexicon is indicative of our original favourite subject matter. I have even gone one further, suggesting that the subconscious receptacle for these original connections still feeds the conscious minds, indirectly, of each new generation as it apprehends the lexicon both consciously at the superficial (surface) level, and simultaneously at the subconscious level beneath, where the thought patterns flow free and unconstrained by too much language. Down there is the bubble-up element in our mental makeup, humanity's muse, our musings, out of the reach of Mrs Grundy and hard to control. You can see I do not hesitate to intrude upon what is fully psychological and am quite ready to ignore the psychological clap trap of the academic psycho brigade under their various determinations. Freud was on drugs all his life and snuffed so much his nose had to be rebuilt. His was a yellow submarine psychology. Dr. Goebbels had a far more practical political and ideological kind of psychology which has held the European constitution in the grip of his Nazi ideology ever since 1950 when Nazism took over Europe again.

So far as the subconscious is concerned, it appears to be a halfway house, not wholly unconscious and inaccessible to the conscious mind as the autonomic system appears to be, but not normally recognised by the waking mind. We can remember some of our dreams and can day dream when dozing, but we lose contact with their sourcing when we consciously address them, left only with the shell without the kernel. It is this kernel which I believe Lithic language roots show to be in certain aspects sovereign. Even when awake we can get some shocking promptings from down below, our muse presenting to the waking mind meanings we never intended, triggered by who knows what or how it happens. I have already attempted to sketch spectral lines in the mental curriculum, Psi, Phi, Pi and Ro. Some or all of Psi, the intentional element anyway, originates in the subconscious, outside intentional control. It is a funnel vapouring up strange concatenations from the deeper levels of the mind. Lithic language roots are just one small part of these vapourings. In passing, the fascination of hallucinatory drugs arises in part from the apparent entrée they provide to this area of hyper-vivid primitive and mostly visual perceptions, mixed with a good deal of giddy swirling sometimes appearing yellow and submarine; but in greater part from the relaxation provided by intoxication, surrender to non-thought. Mental poisoning, it turns out, starts out as fun – courtesy of Psi. The audio frequencies of articulation are more effortful and significant than the visual and are blurred out by artificial stimulants; but their sober research is the more rewarding. That leaves tunes, threnodies which flow with rhythm, somewhere in the middle, redolent of the subconscious muse, opening channels to the inarticulate dream-time, dumping the linguistic impedimenta.

We have now introduced the two ideas of the original discriminatory distinction (d), celebrating the boundary between two different textures on the one hand, which went on to generate in the mind the straight line criterion or continuum (c); and on the other hand the unitary bounded area (d') which was then presented by d, as the prying eye of the infant closed the boundary around a nugget. For long this d' must have been a difficult concept for the inarticulate adjectival mind, texturing its universe in an overwhelming and kaleidoscopic avalanche of perceptions, with no mental handrail or any fixed points to guide it. In such a mass or mess it must surely have seemed superogative to go picking out individual nuggets (nouns) as well. Before speech was added the mind undoubtedly roamed somewhat more freely across its experimental inputs. It is useless to pretend there was no mental activity before speech. Squirrel Nutkin disproves it. But the activity was speechless, it could not make use, as we do now, of the conceptual code we find in words. So there were no stepping stones across the mental abyss. In this fix distincta appeared adjectival, popping up all over. Qualities were not entified or separately located. Adjectival terms answer to more or less, their application slipping into the form of a continuum. In this way the continuum virus was fed into the distinction fold; and the category was thus provided with bogus positive and negative poles. The next question we must ask therefore is what senses aided thinking in the absence of language; and the answer must surely be the visual sense. As the eye discerned the world around so the mind discerned the terms in which to think. We have been focusing our thinking ever more closely ever since, with language thinking in nuggets and labelling them, just as the world goes, and then labelling the labels, and so on and so on. It therefore might be possible, it occurred to me, to find traces of the prior thinking patterns when it came to the birth of language. In other words, I accept the view that the development of language followed upon the thinking needed to get it started. Latterly individuals may use vocabulary to stimulate thought but this is a later development. It is hard to believe that language was created from nothing, after all. We must have thought before we thought to speak.

Surprisingly, it then turned out, and only after years skirting and skating around the idea, that the very patterns I had chosen in illustration of the eye's analysis of its original journeys of discovery do in fact appear to represent quite well some of the first informing meanings of primitive language roots. I turned my attention to the thought patterns I had drawn and deliberately attempted to label them in Lithic terms. It proved a highly educational exercise. The exercise is here repeated, without a great deal of reconsideration or review, but pretty well as it first occurred to me, with only minor re-ordering for clarity in following through the sequential stages of development of the thinking, my originals having been scribbled across the bottom of a page wherever they would fit in, in some degree of excitement.

We start with the criterion tidied to a simple line. I labelled this Pa, because I already had it in mind in company with the burgeoning side developments rounding out. There is a switch between where the outcome of the thinking has led to the "x" and "not x" balloons usurping the labels of the burgeoning process. The finality of the mental process is recognised where Bai, the burgeoning, has changed to the unmarked Ba, flesh, now substantial categories. Here the logic of the pa label is reinforced as the thinned surface tangent of the burgeoned Ba, just as Pa skin is the thinned derivative tangential to ba flesh. A single burgeon may now be abstracted as exemplar of the principal semantic content of the phoneme Ba. The cleavage - from flaking flints, where the effortful strike was taken to sound like "Ka" and the resultant cleavage as the flake was, as it were, spat out, was taken to be like the lesser dental plosive Ta., our letter T today. The sound T was identified as the snap of a stick for the hearth, when the stick became two, one bit in each hand. It can represent the two dimensions of the surface of a flat world, or even the dimensions of space and time. It also is the symbol Two, and its arms make three rays, the ta- rays, ta-rai, or three. Finally there was space for the world in Egyptian, Taun, for which the glyph is a semicircle or 0 divided in two. It provides an opportunity to remark again that Egyptologists have mistaken the glyphs for heaven pt, which they pronounce pet for a bun. It is really pronounced pai-taun, roof of the world and means heaven. The under half is Dua Taun, the second world of the dead and the dead sun as it passes under the earth (which was taken to be a disc), gestating in darkness each night before its rebirth on the Eastern horizon each day. The Dua Taun or Second World is thought to be the meaningless Dwat in academic circles, just a name for Hades, the land of the dead.

Bearing in mind the abstraction of a single line from a crooked boundary is already a recognition of such as representing a continuum too (because both are just lines), it struck me "Pa" and "Ta" might well be treated as serving as markers for the two directions on this line of double derivation, and so as nodes, apt in turn to be identified as male on top and female thereunder. These labels are elementary Lithic phonemes, not yet words as we understand them, it must be remembered. There is still a good deal of unstructured swirling in the Lithic mind. We are shaping our thinking and then giving utterance to the labelling. There is a paradox when we subject this to present day customary thinking, because we regard words for things as simples, and abstract shapes and concepts as a posteriori, whereas I am turning it the other way about. The explanation of the paradox is simple: our customary thinking, after aeons of language, tongue wagging in effect, is wrong. We thought in shapes before we thought in words. There is a good deal of evidence, from primitive science, that subjective minds still thought mostly in shapes even after their tongues had been wagging for a comparatively long time. This almost comes to saying before we spoke we mathematicised. Thinking was that difficult, and there was no notation. So the math of course stayed simple. Some of the evidence is scratched on rocks as symbols for which anthropologists and archaeologists have been searching for crudities as meanings, without success. Spirals are perhaps the pathetic mementos of the whirligigs of the giddy untutored mind trying to home in on a definition but finding a purchase unobtainable, the whorl its only utterance. Cups are similarly abrasions from dizzy screwing with a hard stone or flint to uncover the essential shape it presented, Adam delving, the product of frustrated mind seeking to relieve its emptiness, to pattern the inane, to escape the nausea. Aesthetes can derive comfortable backing from some of this: here was man the artist while still in his birthday suit expressing himself in primitive art forms before his mind was pinched and trammelled by repressive civilisation. But I see these signs as simply cries of pain, like the mentally disturbed rocking back and forth, or the severely religious similarly in traumatic confrontation with their god.

Consider the ongoing development of Pa on its own account. It does not curl round. It can only repeat itself extending sideways. This after all quite precisely copies the movements of the eye in panning or scanning any scene, particularly a whole panorama, which is simply Greek for the pan or whole coverage of what the eye (Ra from the Egyptian) consumes (Ma from the Lithic) or takes in. Pa has been identified already as tangential to Ba, the burgeoning (fleshy) bits. The surface is therefore skin; with the phonetics (Pa the thinned diminutive of Ba as skin or surface) making it a triangulation, surely enough to convince an ox – or a hominid – once presented. So surfaces, we now know, comprise extensions in two dimensions, a Tau or T. Clearly Pa is replicable in both directions like Ba, not just in one direction. The Tau shows the two dimensions of any surface; and there are two more dimensions, space and time, which it is sometimes taken to represent also; as well as the idea of two in the first place. I rather fancy the semantic root of three in turn is from the Rays of the Tau, from the taurai, the tau's rays, there are three. Alas, another dialectical intrusion with mystical connotations for musing about. The wise old owl, speaking in Lithic, would howl "terwit terwoo". Howling already has an i, an a and a u (the h was a Cockney h separating two consecutive vowels, one of which is then apt to be dropped in colloquial speech. In the case of the owl's hoot the h was doing double duty, for trauma and for cockney duty together). Ter wit ter wau, is very wise and very doubly wise, for witches who can read it. For long, witchcraft was a poor man's Marxism, stuck with their dialectic, mind and matter in a crazy waltz together. Can we draw the parallel: Marxism as the modern man's witchcraft? The Egyptian owl, by the way, was a more down to earth bird and spoke a different coarser lingo, saying "Aa-Mahoo", Always all the Ma, viz down, darkness and death in Egyptian. He was a nocturnal marauder, and the Mau (all the Mas) fixed him later in glyph as the bird for alphabetic M, and he is a lot easier to draw than a vulture.

The sun was reborn into our Taun to blaze afresh in the sky like Osiris (really Au Sarai in the original Egyptian, Universal/Eternal Sunrise, promising rebirth after death for all, like the Christian God later). The original prototypical roof for Semites in the desert was made of goatskins. The divided unity can be drawn both halves together, it can even be unity dividing, and thus a parturition, in which case the O might be taken as the birth canal. The birth canal opens and rounds out to pass the head of the infant in a truly astonishing manner - and they say it hurts - bound to have caught the attention of our simple forebears. The Egyptian Aton, which the Egyptologists think is the disc of the sun, is really the Aa-ta-oon, the Everlasting-Birth-Canal, the sun which is born from the dark Dua Taun at Dawn and dies diving into the sea at dusk, both birthing light into the world at sunrise each day, and dowsing the light at night. Perhaps there should be a pause here to explain this ancient poetry. The Egyptian mind in ancient times saw the world as a peep show with successive scenes presented, and these repetitive becomings they articulated as repetitive births, scenic shots. For linguistic purposes, the oo could be the literal round orifice required to make the sound or equally its abstracted signification of totality, in both instances equally using its shape to derive its meanings. The universe was thus for the Egyptians the totality of events rather than the totality of locations we think of today. Their minds were evidently historically different in hundreds of ways, and we shall never know them all.

What I have tried to show is that the mind started out with shapes. I shall be told by academics I have trawled up a whole lot of quite unreliable dream material which can neither be proved nor disproved and it is therefore unscientific, anecdotal (just gossipy) and not worth pursuing. That is why I have included the Egyptian which has linguistic links and the semantics are therefore open to debate, proof or disproof. It may be the material is less unreliable than unwelcome to academics bent on teaching their own concoctions based on rather different semantic prepossessions. In any case, every one of the linguistic connections should properly be taken into account before deciding they are insufficient to provide a convincing statistical base of correlations. All of science is in reality ultimately statistical. Those who decline to be persuaded of the validity of the linguistic points of contact with the semantic catenas worked out in this study of Lithic should be asked to devise another arbitrary scheme of their own as complex and wide ranging in scope without anything to do with Lithic, which can exhibit anyway near a similar number of points of contact with language today, in order to show the Lithic correspondences worthless as they claim. Or even to just name two such points they know already!

The central mystery is still how the synapses in the brain come to prompt for the ideas in the mind. It is hard to see how any electronic state of play can at the same time simply be an idea. Recently an indication was vouchsafed me when expensive new digital hearing aids I bought recently, far more powerful than NHS ones, restored sensitivity to a range of higher notes which had been missing for me for very many years, blurring many of the consonants beyond recognition, since I had the misfortune to get blown up while still quite young and had both my ear drums blown in. These magic modern machines immediately reintroduced much of the missing frequencies but the brain no longer knew how to interpret them. Were they sounds or something else? It took months (but not many) to recover the full proper audio-responses to the inputs of sounds from the hearing aids, so that the dawn chorus came fully back to life and the consonants lined themselves up once more with the utterances with which speech presented me. The translation of the raw signals and the brain's responses to them to picture, sound, idea, etc is by no means a simple matter, it is a skill which has to be learned. The skill is mysterious and subconscious and perhaps it will always remain so. With old age I have quite largely lost the skill and hearing again. The dawn chorus has sunk back to one or two faint chirrups with my hearing aid turned up to full power.

Meanwhile it is not irrational to conduct research just as if there actually were a little manikin in there monitoring the brain's performance. The mind has those characteristics in its own performance precisely, learning as it goes along. For all practical purposes there is a virtual ghost in the machine, anyway as long as the machine stays alive, doing its thinking for it. You can not stuff the mind into the brain (as we understand it). It won't go. Maybe it is the brain which needs to go back to the drawing board, and the cognitive linguistics buffs along with it. The mind is not a thing of any kind at all, it is just a shorthand for all our thinking, an abstract term, the bag for all your thoughts, nothing but actions, an abstraction.

Lightning Source UK Ltd.
Milton Keynes UK
UKHW011105020622
403880UK00009B/432